THE GOURMET GARDENER

THE GOURMET GARDENER

GROWING CHOICE FRUITS AND VEGETABLES WITH SPECTACULAR RESULTS

E. ANNIE PROULX

Illustrations by Robert Byrd

FAWCETT COLUMBINE • NEW YORK

A Fawcett Columbine Book
Published by Ballantine Books

Copyright © 1987 by E. Annie Proulx
Illustrations copyright © 1987 by Robert Byrd

Library of Congress Catalog Card Number: 85-90872

ISBN: 0-449-90227-7

Cover photo by George Kerrigan
Cover design by James R. Harris
Interior design by Michaelis/Carpelis Design Assoc., Inc.

Manufactured in the United States of America
First Edition: March 1987
10 9 8 7 6 5 4 3 2 1

Contents

INTRODUCTION

North Americans have fallen in love with exotic fruits and vegetables, and gardeners have started collecting heirloom cultivars and odd edible plants as they once collected stamps or china dogs:

- One of the country's largest produce wholesalers, Pedi Brothers, outside of Chicago, handles 2,800 kinds of vegetables, fruits, and nuts: kiwi, gingerroot, bitter orange, Seckel pear, cherries, ugli fruit, alfalfa sprouts, celeriac, a dozen kinds of chiles, chayote, jicama, pie pumpkins, yellow zucchini, Munich beer radishes, Cos lettuce, radicchio, almonds, chestnuts, guavas, melons, herbs, beets, winter melon, bamboo shoots, taro, papaya, and on and on and on.

- The produce sections of supermarkets have expanded again and again until many aisles of perishable fresh produce in a vivid palette of colors tempt customers to try. Some of this good stuff is locally grown.

- Ethnic restaurants and food shops have become big business as people rush to enjoy Creole cooking or chiles rellenos or wild-rice shoots. Epicurean restaurants specializing in fine cuisine offer customers celeriac vinaigrette, salads of forced witloof chicory or red Italian radicchio, Portuguese *couve tronchuda*, and dozens of other regional delicacies that were flown in from abroad until the last few years.

- Farmers' markets are springing up everywhere, stalls and baskets brimming with dew-fresh tomatoes, apples, squash, melons, and potatoes. These open-air markets can be found in all parts of North America from Alaska to Vermont, from British Columbia to Montreal, from Tampa to Duluth.

- Breeders have turned their attention to disease-resistant cultivars with good flavor, whereas they once concentrated on brightly colored appearance and shipping strength.

● Specialty seed houses concentrating on European and oriental garden delights have been buried in orders from enthusiastic gardeners who want outstanding flavors and sublime textures rather than gargantuan size or neon color for their tables.

The gourmet gardener wants specialties and excellent flavor. This gardener dreams of fragrant, deep-fleshed melons eaten minutes after they are slipped from the vine; of russeted ocher apples with curious names that are not sold in any store but that conceal beneath their rough skin a delicate yellow flesh reminiscent of honey and almond cream; of black beans for the ineffable soup of the same name; blue corn for the old, authentic tortillas; damask roses for rose-petal jelly and culinary rosewater; deertongue lettuces remembered from grandfather's garden; jicama sliced thin and eaten with lime juice and salt. There is no more fascinating pleasure than running down the sources of seeds and rootstocks for the special cultivars one fancies and then growing them for an unforgettable eating experience. There is no substitute—neither culinary skill nor rare produce—for garden-ripened, fresh, fresh, fresh vegetables and fruits gathered by the gardener's own hand.

This book is for the gardener who wishes to find sources of unusual and outstanding fruits and vegetables and to grow them in the home garden. It is a guide to the choicest and finest-flavored cultivars and their culture. Specialty seed dealers are given here, nurseries that carry uncommon fruits, associations that allow gardeners to participate in developing new cultivars, makers of and dealers in fine tools[*], and books on special aspects of gardening for the kitchen[†]. Because knowing something of a domestic plant's wild past both interests and aids the gardener, some history of the vegetables and fruits listed here is included. Many of the plants described will be unfamiliar to the backyard gardener, but all of them, with a few exceptions, can be grown in a temperate climate. The tropical-fruit cultivars listed here can be successfully grown either indoors or in the greenhouse. Part of the pleasure in fine gardening, as in fine dining, lies in trying the unfamiliar and exotic. Another pleasure lies in striving for the best quality and flavors. Here is an introduction to both these delights.

---

[*]Addresses of sources are listed at the back of the book, p. 179.
[†]See lists throughout and the bibliography, p. 183.

THE GOURMET GARDENER

GARDENING TECHNIQUES FOR GOURMET VEGETABLES AND FRUITS

THE NEW KITCHEN GARDENING

A new kind of gardening has become part of our lives. It is experimental, specialized, nostalgic, and beautiful when edible plants are part of the aesthetic landscape. The new gardening parallels our awakened interest in fine food, regional delicacies, and native cooking—the hot local chiles handed down from generation to generation in the Southwest, New England deep-dish apple pie made with Pinkham Pie apples or greenings. We have developed a taste for the choice and unusual products of the garden, first sampled on travels that may range from neighboring counties to the other side of the world. Lotus root, rat-tailed radishes, *fraises des bois*, French horticultural beans, Mexican blue corn, flowering Chinese chives, and Italian arugula are a few of the vegetables included in our plots.

Instead of the large, rectangular row garden of the past, where drier, dense "keeper" vegetables were grown for quantity and winter storage rather than flavor, we now plant several small gardens of individual character. Hard by the ornamental perennial beds we grow the salad garden, the herb garden, the experimental bed where we try new cultivars and exotic imports, the water garden, the berry and asparagus beds, the little orchard of a few choice fruit trees. We walk in our vegetable and fruit gardens with friends as people of another age walked among the roses and topiary. We save the seeds of old and rare cultivars and exchange them for others. We collect different kinds of turnips or unusual tomatoes or heirloom beans. We put gardens in sun-rooms and solar additions, on rooftops, under skylights and on balconies, on company property or in municipal plots, in backyards and on steep hillsides.

It is an exciting time to be gardening, a period of explosive interest in finer vegetables, piquant taste experiences, and new sources of seed.

Great cooks, caterers, epicurean vegetarians, gourmets, restaurateurs, and hearty trenchermen have always known that the finest experiences at the table are founded on fresh-plucked fruits and vegetables. In Europe many restaurants and inns that set fine tables have kitchen gardens out back supplemented by daily trips to local markets for regional specialities. In this country, the new horticultural enterprise of supplying restaurants with gourmet produce—cultivars of superior flavor and unusual vegetables and fruits, most too delicate for commercial shipping—is growing.

Even a first-time gardener can grow symphonies for the palate. Old hands with the hoe are never done discovering new treasures to grow and better ways to grow them. In this book the focus is on superior flavors and textures, on the choice and the unusual, and on gardening techniques to achieve but one end—the superb gastronomic experience.

HOW TO GROW FINE VEGETABLES AND FRUIT

The Garden Site

A badly placed garden is the reason most crops fail and their owners curse the day they opened a seed catalog. To be able to recognize the right place for the kind of garden you want to grow is to win the opening skirmish in the battle with climate and weather. There's always something wrong with the general conditions: In New England, Alaska, and the mountains, the growing season is too brief; in the South, humidity and heat and insects dampen the spirits; in the Maritimes and the Pacific Northwest, there is too much fog and not enough sunlight; in the Midwest, there is drought and hail; in the Southwest, alkaline soil and scant rainfall. But in all of these places people are growing superb gardens.

United States Department of Agriculture (USDA) zone maps give only the most general indications of a region's climate. Each garden has its own microclimate—an extremely localized mélange of wind, weather, slope, shelter, water and air drainage, length of growing season, temperature averages, and amount of sunlight. Within the garden are even smaller "zones," measured in feet and inches. The microclimates of the backyard can be startlingly different from those marked on the seed-packet map. A good eye for the warm, sheltered spot is what makes it possible for those famous Italian home gardeners in Boston and New York City to bring fig trees to fruit outdoors. They have found microclimates far warmer than the general zone where they live.

Inside the boundaries of the garden itself are small variations in soil type, dryness, temperature fluctuation, and shade that seem negligible to the gardener from his or her lofty height more than five feet above the earth's surface but that may be crucial to the plants expected to grow there. Careful observation and regularly recorded measurements of temperature, pH, and moisture mark the best natural microclimates for your permanent bed sites. This process takes several seasons. One goes ahead and plants in what seems to be the best place, ready to shift plots to a better location as soon as it is revealed.

The seed catalogs tout celeriac, for example, as an easy crop, within the capabilities of any general gardener, but not everyone can grow it. If your monthly mean temperatures during the growing season are higher than 70 to 75 degrees F, the crop is apt to fail or make a poor showing, with only a few tough, ill-flavored tubers. Many vegetables and fruits have similarly stringent requirements of water or pH or sunlight times or nutrients, and the continuing fascination of gardening is discovering these quirks and temperamental crotchets, not only among species but among cultivars within the same species.

The importance of ground-level thermometers and recordkeeping in determining the mean temperature of a garden site was made very clear in a nine-year-long study at the University of Vermont by the late Richard J. Hopp. He discovered significant variations in temperature between a location 7.5 centimeters (about three inches) above the ground and the standard height of an instrument shelter at 150 centimeters. The average date of the last occurrence of spring frost was sixteen days later at ground level than at 150 centimeters; in autumn, the first frosts near the ground came fourteen days earlier than at 150 centimeters. In other words, where Hopp took temperature measurements, the growing season was thirty days shorter at ground level than was indicated by the instruments five feet above them, which were the sources of zone-map data!

Some state experiment stations have ground-level temperature information for selected areas, but it is likely that you will have to set up maximum-minimum thermometers on your garden site at ground level and keep your own records for a few seasons before you truly know the rigors and vagaries of your particular microclimate.

The microclimates of the garden can be improved by dozens of artful tricks. Where wind rakes the plains, fences and windbreaks, walls and trees, can moderate the desiccating, rough flow of air. Scanty rainfall or periods of drought are ameliorated by drip irrigation. Early autumn frosts are held away from late-maturing crops by stone walls that hold the heat. The most dramatic alteration of microclimates in the garden comes with use of cold frames, continuous glass cloches, and plastic tunnels in early and late frost periods. Sometimes it seems to the traveler that all of England in March is under glass, coaxing along the little lettuces.

GOOD GARDEN SITES

Most people have an instinctive sense of the right place for their garden or soon develop one. Here's a checklist of what to look for:

- **Loamy, fertile soil (this can be made over time)**
- **At least six hours of daily sunlight (seacoast gardeners, look twice)**
- **A steady supply of adequate water during the growing season**
- **Close proximity to house for convenience and pleasure**
- **A size you can handle enjoyably, but with room to grow the plants you like**
- **A gentle slope for good air and water drainage**
- **A fence or wall to provide shelter from the elements, protection from animals and thieves, and privacy for the gardener**

Over the years, garden sites can be improved and tailored to the particular needs of the plants that grow there. Experience, observation, trial and error, and ongoing experimentation make fine gardens, but the shrewd choice of a garden site can allow you to grow delicacies that gardeners a hundred miles to the south would hesitate to try.

The Garden Path

Garden paths are important. Brick or stone laid in the paths makes pleasanter, cleaner walking, and the soil does not compact under the foot. Plant roots will extend under a brick wall and utilize the space, nutrients, and extra moisture, but a hard-trodden path makes a barrier underground that few roots can penetrate.

The Crucial Importance of Good Soil

Tender, fine-fleshed, aromatic, and richly flavored fruits and vegetables need an environment made up of good soil, adequate water and sunlight, the right nutrients, and room to grow. Fabulous gardens have been grown in desert and beach sand; on rocky, thin-soiled mountain slopes; in swampy muck; and in hard-pan clay—after the nightmare soils were improved. The ideal is fertile, loamy soil, but hardly anyone starts out with such a choice growing medium. The basis of all successful gardening since the days of slash-and-burn agriculture is improving the soil, even if it takes years to make something decent out of flimsy sand or dense, sticky clay.

In the last few decades North American gardeners have come a long way. There are hundreds of thousands of experienced gardeners around who use sophisticated techniques to grow crops of high quality. They've learned how to condition poor soils with compost and rotted manures; to sample and test soils; to adjust the acidic soils of New England by adding lime and the alkaline soils of the Southwest by very gradually working in organic material; to balance out soil fertility by growing green manures, rotating crops, and applying specific amounts of deficient elements. Cold soils can be warmed in early spring with sheets of clear plastic, and thick mulches keep the same soil cool and moist in the root zone during torrid summer heat.

Soil does four major things for plants: (a) It anchors the roots and gives the plant support; (b) it supplies the plant with water; (c) it carries the minerals plants need for growth; and (d) it holds soil air for the roots. The ideal soil performs these four tasks with equal efficiency.

Soil classification as done by professional agriculturalists can be tremendously complex and technical, but most home gardeners judge soils simply by texture. The ideal growing medium is a friable loam with a good crumb and tilth. A friable soil is one that crumbles easily when pressed with a finger; *tilth* refers to soil texture. Loam is made up of a fairly even mix of three basic soil types: clay, silt, and sand. If any one of these soils dominates the mix, we speak of a sandy loam or a clay loam or a silt loam.

Sand is made up of relatively large particles that range in size from .05 to

2 millimeters (mm). Silt is much smaller, with an average particle size of only .002 to .05 mm. Both sand and silt are nothing but broken-down rock fragments, and both are chemically inert compared with clay. Their importance in a garden soil is to give it structure and body, something like the tannin in wines.

Clay is a horse of a different color and by far the most important of the soil types to the gardener, for the microscopically tiny particles (less than .002 mm) are electrically charged and can collect and hold on their surfaces the nutrients needed by plants. Clay particles are platelike in shape and have a million times more surface area than an equal volume of sand.

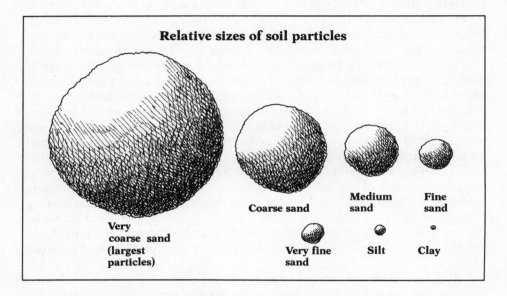

Relative sizes of soil particles

Very coarse sand (largest particles)

Coarse sand

Very fine sand

Medium sand

Silt

Fine sand

Clay

Yet clay soils are slippery, stiff, and dense. They are hard to dig and slow to drain. Clay soil tends to be acidic because of this poor drainage, and it hardens into a surface crust that imprisons seedlings. It can be so dense that roots have difficulty penetrating it. Worst of all, although clay soils are high in nutrients, their low pH may chemically bond the nutrients to the clay particles, preventing the hungry plants from receiving any nourishment.

But a clay soil built up to a loam by the gardener is a marvelous medium for plants. Loam soil contains silts, sand, and clay particles in equal proportions. It has good drainage yet retains enough moisture to satisfy plants. The aeration is good, and plenty of nutrients are handy in useable form. This versatile, healthy mixture is the basic stuff of the gourmet garden, the necessary medium for growing the finest crops. Someone has figured out that a handful of loam contains five to ten acres of surface area, and the astounding root systems of plants put most of that surface area to use. A famous study of the root system of a single winter rye plant showed 2 million feet, or 380 miles, of root system packed into two cubic feet of soil.

The importance of growing your vegetables in this fertile, loamy stuff cannot be overstated, for only in this medium can they become juicy, flavorful fruits of the best texture. Garden plants must grow quickly and steadily in order to reach perfection. In good soil and with adequate water, they can reach that ideal.

The attentions of the gardener make a profound difference in the structure of the soil. Those attentions include liming; adding compost, manure, and other organic material; improving drainage; and tilling or working the soil. Tilling the soil does not mean running a rototiller up and down the rows. In fact, studies have shown that both plowing and rototilling have an adverse effect on soil structure over time, breaking down the aggregate clumps of soil particles and pounding the soil a few inches below the surface into a hard "plow-pan" layer down below that is nearly as hard as concrete. A new gardening technique that avoids these problems is a combination of double digging, followed by minimum tillage in following years and heavy mulches. Minimum tillage works best with soil that is in good physical condition and has good tilth.

Organic Material

Adding organic material to a poor soil to improve it, or to a soil already supporting plants to keep it in decent shape, has wonderful effects. Important microorganisms are added to the soil, nutrient levels are boosted, water retention capacity is improved, and the soil structure and tilth are renewed. The best soil improver is decomposed organic material or *humus*, the end result of composting. Humus is a superb companion to clay particles.

Crop rotations that include legumes help keep organic-material levels high in a soil (see pp. 17–19). *Green-manuring*, or turning under certain green crops while they are still immature, builds soil, because immature plants break down very rapidly. (Some of the more common green manures are crimson clover, vetch, buckwheat, rye, soybeans.) Farm manure, which is made up mostly of undigested plant parts, adds some nutrients and improves tilth. However, nearly all manures are low in phosphorus, an essential element for plants.

SOME COMMONLY USED GREEN-MANURE CROPS

Green Manures	Areas for Which Best Adapted					When to Sow	When to Turn Under
	N.E. and N.C. States	Southern and S.E. States	Gulf Coast and Florida	Northwestern States	Southwestern States		
Legumes						When to Sow	When to Turn Under
Soybeans	●	●	●	●	●	Spring or summer	Summer or fall
Crimson clover	●	●	●	●	●	Fall	Spring
Cowpea		●	●		●	Late spring or early summer	Summer or fall
Crotalaria		●	●		●	Spring or summer	Summer or fall
Indigo, hairy		●	●		●	Spring or early summer	Summer or fall
Lespedeza		●				Early spring	Summer or fall
Field pea	●	●	●	●	●	Early spring	Summer
Sweet clover	●	●	●	●	●	Spring	Summer
Vetch (hairy or common)	●	●	●	●	●	Spring or fall	Fall or spring
Nonlegumes							
Barley	●			●	●	Spring or fall	Summer or spring
Buckwheat	●			●		Late spring and summer	Summer or fall
Millet	●					Late spring or summer	Summer or fall
Oats	●	●	●	●	●	Spring or fall	Summer, spring, or fall
Rye, spring	●	●				Spring	Summer
Rye, winter	●	●				Fall	Spring
Sudan grass	●	●	●	●	●	Late spring or summer	Summer or fall
Wheat, winter	●			●		Fall	Spring

Courtesy of U.S. Department of Agriculture

pH—The Mystery Unfolded

Soil pH refers to a measurement of alkalinity or acidity in a logarithmic instead of an arithmetic progression. A soil that has a pH of 6.5 is ten times as acidic as one with a pH of 6.6. If a soil with a pH of 5.5 is compared with the 6.5 soil, it proves to be a hundred times more acidic. A knowledge of soil pH is important to gardeners, because it directly affects the availability of nutrients to the garden plants. At a pH lower than 5, iron, zinc, manganese, copper, and cobalt are most available to plants. When the pH is above 5, molybdenum, potassium, calcium, and magnesium become more available. The very important element phosphorus has a narrow range of availability, from pH 6 to pH 7. So vital is phosphorus to plants that garden-soil pH recommendations from soil scientists have focused on the familiar pH 6.5 as ideal, the optimum point of phosphorus availability. The plants will generally manage to get some of what they need of the other nutrients, but phosphorus is life itself.

Every plant species enjoys a particular pH range in which it most easily takes in nutrients, but because of the phosphorus range, almost all vegetables do pretty well from 6.0 to 6.5. Acid soils, unless corrected, can make

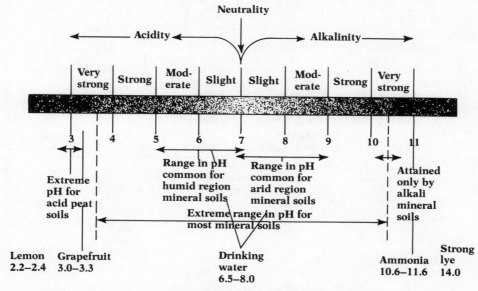

A portion of the pH scale, and the pH's of some soils and common household products.

Reprinted with permission of Macmillan Publishing Co., Inc., from Nyle C. Brady, The Nature and Properties of Soils. *Copyright © 1974 Macmillan Publishing Co., Inc.*

vegetable development difficult or impossible. Precisely why acid soils hurt plants is not known, but certain deficiencies and toxicities seem to be linked to the problem. Phosphates and microorganisms become inactive in acid soil; calcium and magnesium deficiencies are common; toxic effects from aluminum and manganese show up. Aluminum toxicity can devastate beets and celery. Manganese poisoning is deadly to beans and cole crops.

Not all soils are acid. Saline and sodic soils, which are common in the semi-arid Southwest and in Alberta and Saskatchewan, characterize millions of acres of land in North America. These conditions develop when soil moisture evaporates rapidly and leaves an accumulation of salts in the upper strata of soil. Saline soils, with their high levels of soluble salts, are called *white alkali soils* because the salts give them a pale, dusty appearance, as anyone who has ever traveled through the West has noted. Sodic soils, which contain high sodium levels, are called *black alkali* because the sodium carries dark humus up to the soil surface.

Both saline and sodic soils can pull moisture out of a plant's roots and

TOLERANCE OF VEGETABLE CROPS TO SALTY SOIL

High Salt Tolerance	Medium Salt Tolerance		Low Salt Tolerance
Garden beet	Tomato	Potato	Radish
Kale	Broccoli	Carrot	Celery
Asparagus	Cabbage	Onion	Green bean
Spinach	Bell pepper	Pea	
Sugar beet	Cauliflower	Squash	
	Lettuce	Cucumber	
	Sweet corn	Sunflower	

TOLERANCE OF FRUIT CROPS TO SALTY SOIL

High Salt Tolerance	Medium Salt Tolerance	Low Salt Tolerance	
Date palm	Fig	Pear	Almond
	Olive	Apple	Apricot
	Grape	Orange	Peach
	Cantaloupe	Grapefruit	Strawberry
		Prune	Lemon
		Plum	Avocado

Courtesy of U.S. Department of Agriculture

may be concentrated enough to actually eat away plant tissue. These soils tend to puddle and bake to a hard, platelike texture.

Some plants are tolerant of saline soils, few of sodic soils. Gardeners plagued with these conditions learn to plant cultivars that can take saline, such as beets, kale, asparagus, spinach, and sugar beet, and to avoid those that are very sensitive to salts, such as celery, green beans, strawberries, almonds, peaches, and radishes.

Mulching helps retard evaporation and accumulation of salts. In extreme cases of saline soil, gardeners may have to install drainage tiles and flush the salts out of the soil with good, nonsaline water. This can be an expensive procedure where there are water shortages and high water costs. Local soil experts are indispensable in solving saline or sodic soil problems. Many gardeners have worked hard improving such soils and ferreting out native plant crops suited to them. It's worth the effort.

Soil test kits and directions for taking a good sample that will yield accurate readings are available from county agents. The samples are tested at state university laboratories at a modest cost in most states.

There are a growing number of private soil-testing laboratories that will do far more detailed analyses, including tests for micronutrients and trace elements. These tests, which can cost five times as much as the state lab tests, give detailed prescriptions to remedy soil problems and will draw up soil correction programs to improve the garden soil over a long period.

The soil test, whether a six-dollar one at the state lab or an expensive fifty-dollar test at a private lab, will tell you how much of what to add to your particular soil. Guesswork, the random dumping of ashes or lime to "sweeten" the soil, the addition of trace minerals you suspect are needed, can be mistakes that take seasons to correct. The home gardener can't do an accurate soil test; you need a lab.

Three important soil-testing laboratories are:
Woods End Laboratory
RFD Box 65
Temple, Maine 04984

S. R. Sorensen, Prescription Soil Analysis
Box 80631
Lincoln, Nebraska 68501

Eaton Valley Agricultural Services
C.P. 25
Sawyerville, Quebec, Canada J0B 3A0

Nutrients—Food of the Plants

Plants must get certain essential elements. Six major elements, usually referred to in gardening jargon as *macronutrients*, are nitrogen, phosphorus, potassium, calcium, magnesium, and sulfur. Of these, three are so important they are called primary, and a bag of commercial fertilizer that contains these three—nitrogen, phosphorus, and potassium—is optimistically called a complete fertilizer.

The big three are abbreviated NPK: N for nitrogen, P for phosphorus, and K for potassium. NPK numbers on a bag of fertilizer represent percentages, so that 10-20-10, for example, means that the contents of the bag are 10 percent nitrogen, 20 percent phosphorus, and 10 percent potassium. The remaining 60 percent is filler.

Nitrogen helps plants make good growth in leaves, stems, flowers, and fruits. It is essential in helping the plant form protein and gives plants their green color. Low nitrogen levels can show up in yellowed leaves, but too much can kill plants. Good sources of nitrogen are immature green manure/legume crops turned into the soil; meals made from blood, hoof, horn, fish, soybean, or cottonseed; poultry manure, guano, sodium nitrate, and tankage. Among garden plants, only legumes can fix nitrogen in the soil, though this ability is known to occur in six or more plant families, including certain cacti. Alfalfa is without peer in fixing atmospheric nitrogen in the soil. Peas and beans fix only a fifth as much nitrogen per acre as alfalfa, even when the entire plants are turned under. Because gardeners have a curious tendency to harvest most of their pea and bean crops, not much is left to work into the soil. Garden legumes, then, are considered to be conservators of nitrogen rather than realistic sources of increase or nitrogen fixing.

Phosphorus, as we have seen, is absolutely vital to plants, for they use it in the cell division process. It makes strong roots, builds up the plant's disease resistance, and aids fruit setting. Stunted, sparsely fruited plants may be languishing from phosphorus deficiency. Sources are phosphate rock, clay-base soft phosphate, steamed and raw bone meal, and tankage.

Potassium, called *potash* by many, is linked with key chemical processes in a plant's early stages of growth and development. Potassium builds strong stems and root systems. Sources available to gardeners are kelp, greensand, poultry manure, wood ash, and powdered granite.

Calcium, magnesium, and sulfur, all present in farm manures, are secondary elements and need to be replenished in the soil often. The micronutrients—iron, manganese, boron, molybdenum, copper, zinc, chlorine and cobalt—are found in most soils, except in certain localities where years of taking off the crops without replenishing the soil has created deficiencies. Micronutrients are used by plants in tiny traces, and the state lab test doesn't bother to measure these unless they are specifically requested. It is not a good idea to guess that plant illnesses and problems are linked to nutrient deficiencies and to start adding supposed missing elements unless you have had a soil test and follow the prescription for bringing the soil back into balance.

TO MAKE MANURE TEA

Set an empty barrel in or near the garden. Dump in cow, rabbit, or horse manure, filling the barrel one-third full. Fastidious gardeners prefer to put the manure in a burlap sack and the sack in the barrel. Add water to the top of the barrel and let the mixture stand a few days before using it. Ladle out the nutritious liquid, a cupful to a plant, once a week during the growing season. Keep the barrel topped up with water.

Compost

Composting is the ancient gardening procedure of deliberately stockpiling organic material, letting it decay, then adding it to the garden or field. Leftover vegetable matter from the garden, kitchen scraps of fruit and vegetable peelings, rotten produce, old dried flowers, manure and soil, and sometimes a little limestone make up the layers of the compost pile. Grass clippings, leaves, twigs, and nearly anything that will break down into humus goes onto the compost pile. Humus is the end product, a roaring colony of microbiotic life highly beneficial to soil and plants. Wear stout shoes when working around the compost pile and keep your tetanus shots up-to-date.

In the last fifty years or so, composting has been glorified as an innovative and indispensable gardening technique; however, the general idea has been practiced for centuries. Compost is not a complete fertilizer, but it is a superb soil conditioner. Certain elements and/or manure may still have to be added to a well-composted garden. In some soils, such as semiarid alkaline soils, large amounts of organic material added all at once can actually exacerbate the soil salinity. The organic material does indeed make the soil more porous and fluffy, but the increased porosity pulls up salts from below, and rapid evaporation then concentrates the salts in the root zone, with unpleasant effects on the plants. The trick is to add the organic material slowly, over a period of years, and to reduce evaporation by using mulches. Compost piles are built on a layer of branches in order to allow oxygen to get into the pile. Layers of grass clippings, young weeds without seeds, barn manure—nearly anything vegetative—will decay into rich, black humus. As soon as the humus is a mellow, crumbly, friable mass, it should be worked into the garden soil. You can leave a compost pile too long. Then it seems to disappear into the soil below the bin.

NO GOOD FOR THE COMPOST PILE

- **No toxic plant material (poison ivy or oak, black walnut, oleander, castor bean, eucalyptus, and so on).**
- **No weeds that have developed seeds. Beware cockleburs; you may toss the plants with green, barely developed seedpods or "burs" (each bur contains two seeds) on the compost pile, thinking them too young to cause trouble—alas, the seed will mature right in the pile.**
- **No gray water (bathtub, sink, rinse, barn, etc. water) nor cat, dog, or human manure. All contain harmful pathogens that may resist the pile's heat.**
- **No grease, fat, or detergent; they will not break down.**
- **No old magazines, junk mail, or color-printed paper; inks contain toxic metals.**
- **No diseased or insect-laden plant material**

Garden Plans—Who Needs Them?

Paper garden plans, like garden planting records, are truly indispensable for keeping track of crop rotations. They can control uninhibited seed-packet splurging and bring order to the puzzle of plant pollination requirements and spacing. Tall crops go where they will not shade neighbors, heavy feeders move onto enriched beds. Different planting times for cool-weather or warm-weather crops or second plantings can be noted. Fruit-tree-pollination needs call for paper planning. Corn planted in short-row blocks enjoys a higher pollination rate than a few long rows. If you grow several kinds of corn that cross-pollinate, they must be isolated or they will cross. For example, sweet corn must be kept away from field corn or popcorn. New super-sweet cultivars have to be kept away from older types, lest dominant genes make starchy, tough sweet corn in cross-pollination accidents.

If you are thinking about saving seed, consider cross-pollination between squash family members, between tomato cultivars, carrots, which will cross with wild-carrot relatives, radishes, which also cross with wild members of the family, and all of the *Brassicae*, which cross readily. Seed savers quickly discover that garden plans and good records are the only way to tell what you are doing.

Large block groupings of similar or related plants are attractive because they make figuring out crop rotations simple; you just shuffle the blocks successively around the garden course year after year, like playing green Monopoly. The disadvantage of such monoculture plantings in even a medium-size garden is the greater likelihood of insect and animal damage. Apparently a mass of similar plants growing together, gives off a strong chemical signal that alerts every pest in the county that Gardener George is growing carrots again. But if you intercrop and break up the big blocks into small stands of similar plants interspersed with quite different types, it seems to confuse insect predators, and the result is a greater number of unblemished, wholesome fruits.

Crop Rotation: Number One Gardening Technique

Crop rotation is the heart of good gardening. If crops are shifted annually, the soil stays in good health. Crop yields continue to be abundant instead of slacking off to a few pitiful fruits. Disease and insect damage are minimized. Soils bled of nutrients by plants that feed voraciously are restored with a rotating cover crop.

Potatoes, for example, are very greedy feeders, and will seriously deplete soils of nitrogen if they are planted in the same place year after year. Plant scientists suggest a long rotation of six years for potatoes, and they should be planted where cereal or hay crops have preceded them. A shorter, four-year rotation is possible by planting potatoes in soil where a legume cover crop—preferably alfalfa—has been turned under the preceding season.

Carrots, celery, parsnips, and parsley are hosts to the nasty little carrot rust fly. The pupae hibernate over the winter in the soil, and another host plant sown in that ground the next spring is prey to rust-fly attack, dwarfism, and soft-rot bacteria.

The *Brassicae* are all heavy nitrogen feeders. If you plant cabbage, broccoli, cauliflower, and kale in the same plot each year, the soil will soon be exhausted. The depleted soil will then produce increasingly poor crops, and the serious *Brassica* disease clubroot establishes itself easily in the sick soil.

Verticillium wilt, onion white-rot, scab, blight, wireworm, and nematode infestations are linked to negligent crop rotation.

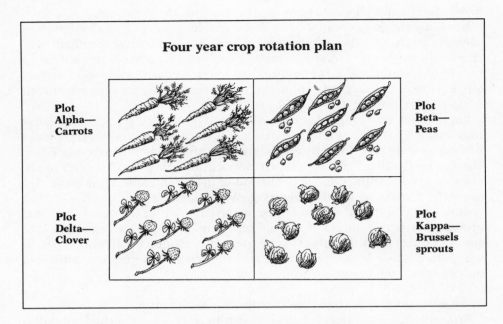

Four year crop rotation plan

Plot Alpha—Carrots

Plot Beta—Peas

Plot Delta—Clover

Plot Kappa—Brussels sprouts

There are many crop rotation plans devised to suit certain crops and particular regions. A good one for the home garden is the classic four-year rotation. In this plan the garden is divided into four plots of equal area. The plants assigned to each section are grouped so that heavy feeders follow light feeders the next season. Here is one simplified scheme:

Plot Alpha: root crops such as carrots, turnips, potatoes, beets, radishes, jicama, celeriac, scorzonera, salsify.

Plot Beta: home for the nitrogen-conserving legumes—Fin de Bagnols, Black Turtle beans, tepary beans, Dwarf Horticultural, Kentucky Wonder beans, chick-peas, snow peas, *petits pois*, Laxton's Progress, and so on.

Plot Kappa: Here are the heavy-feeding cauliflowers, brussels sprouts, cabbages, and other *Brassicae*. Tomatoes, squash, and pumpkins are all heavy feeders, too, and may make up all or part of Plot Kappa.

Plot Delta: The green-manure crop—a legume such as clover, alfalfa, or vetch—plowed under when young.

Every new planting season the gardener rotates the plots clockwise by one plot, so that the nitrogen-conserving beans and peas move onto the plot vacated by the hungry *Brassicae*; these cabbages and their relatives go forward to the rich soil fattened by green manure; the cover crop repairs the soil now where the roots grew the season before, and so on around the garden. It will be four years before repeat crops are grown in the same soil.

Other arrangements are possible. A five- or six-year rotation with vines and other crops worked into the scheme is popular, and where potatoes are one of your garden crops, a six-year rotation is better. Some gardeners, who interplant companion species either to break up a monoculture block or for the benefits of a compatible or protective companion, will have more complicated rotation plans. Records and data stored on your home computer can make crop rotation easier.

Companion Planting

In a sense, crop rotation is companion planting over a long time. It is known, but not yet well understood, that plants release all sorts of chemicals—phenolic acids, organic cyanides, steroids, alkaloids, terpenoids—from their roots into the soil around them and from their leaves into the air. Some of these extracts have been discovered to contain antifungal or antibacterial substances that retard or inhibit seed germination. Black walnut trees release juglone, a very powerful growth inhibitor. Young peach and apple trees, if planted in an orchard where old peach or apple trees grew, will be stunted or deformed or make marginal growth progress. Alfalfa releases chemicals into the soil that inhibit successive crops of alfalfa from growing there. These phenomena may be nature's way of insisting on crop rotation.

CROP ROTATION BASICS

- Leaf crops take nitrogen from the soil, but legumes maintain it.
- Heavy feeders aare succeeded by legume crops.
- Deep-rooted crops should follow up shallow-rooted crops to improve soil tilth and aeration.
- Green manure is the pivot of crop rotation schemes.

There has been a good deal written in popular gardening publications about using specific combinations of plants in the garden to control insect pests by repelling or attracting them. But the scientific community is skeptical about the efficacy of many of the claims. When large plantings of one species are broken into small clusters with other species as nearby neighbors, insect damage is indeed reduced. But this may occur because the muddled-up chemical signals given off by the integrated plants confuse insect pests, not because specific companion plants repel them. The study of the complex biological interactions between plants and insects is one of the newest branches of horticulture, and no one yet really understands why or how companion planting works. The following plants are reported by many gardeners to have a noticeable deterrent action on certain pests:

Marigold	Repels nematodes, bean beetles
Nasturtium	Deters squash bugs, aphids
Rosemary	Deters cabbage moths, carrot rust flies, bean beetles
Onion	Repels many insects
Thyme	Repels cabbage worms

It does no harm, and may help, to work these "companions" into your garden plan.

Gardening Styles

Most gardeners hold the earth and its products in reverence, and for many people gardening goes beyond supplying the table, taking on spiritual and philosophical overtones. For others, what counts is the superior nutritional quality of home-grown produce and the comforting knowledge of its purity and wholesomeness. For others of us the garden is the source of Lucullan repasts, and we plant and harvest for the cutting board, the cooking pot, and the steaming platter. In part, a gardener's techniques and style reflect his or her personal feelings about the growing earth.

Traditionally North Americans have made gardens that are large plots plowed yearly and formed into wide-aisle rows with bare earth exposed. The water supply was left to heaven, and chemical fertilizers were added as a matter of course when yields began to wane. Chemical pesticides to combat the hordes of insects that descended on the convenient rows were sprayed and sprinkled freely. Fruit trees were doused with fungicides as well. The goal was not only fresh vegetables and fruit in season, but big harvests to fill the pantry and cellar. All of this has changed.

New attitudes about what we eat, a concern for the soil and the environment, less room for gardening, and an inclination not to waste growing space have changed a lot of our ideas. Here is a brief review of some of the gardening styles and procedures around today. Many of these overlap. If you are a beginning gardener, you might like to try out several ways of growing things in order to find what suits you best. Experiment with a corner of the main garden or dig a new bed to try out new ways. Keep a few notes to make things clearer.

Organic Gardening

This is humankind's most ancient approach to gardening, bolstered by modern scientific studies. In a nutshell, organic gardening is the successful attempt to grow fruits and vegetables without the aid of synthetic chemical fertilizers, herbicides, or pesticides. Natural "organic" sprays are used with some vulnerable fruits, and many ingenious biological controls against injurious pests—from releasing the eggs of praying mantises in the garden to spraying apple trees with an extract of hot chile pepper—have been worked out to make the least impact on the natural balance of soil, air, and water. Great attention is given to soil improvement and maintenance through the use of organic material as mulches and conditioners, composting, green-manure crops, and animal manures. The double goal is (a) to protect the environment from toxic residues and (b) to produce high-quality, superby flavored fruits and vegetables. Crop rotation and companion planting are practiced as a matter of course.

The Rodale Press in Emmaus, Pennsylvania, is the long-time central source of organic-gardening thought, and more than a million gardeners read the magazine *Organic Gardening* each month.

High-Density Gardening

High-density, or high-yield, gardening has several schools, which tend to overlap with each other and the more general organic approach.

Biodynamic/French Intensive Gardening. This is a combination of two turn-of-the-century horticultural approaches. French Intensive gardening was first practiced on a few acres outside Paris in the 1890s. Strong market demands for out-of-season delicacies, such as lettuce and melons, contributed to the development of these techniques. The lettuces and other crops were grown in extraordinarily rich beds of soil underlaid eighteen inches down with horse manure. The plants were spaced carefully so that leaf margins would just meet and form a dense shade on the soil beneath. The shade slowed down evaporation and checked weed growth. Seedlings were set out in the garden extremely early. The heat from the decomposing horse manure below and the protection of the glass bells, called *cloches*, that covered each plant created very pleasant microclimates. The plants grew rapidly and steadily and were of extremely fine quality, ready to harvest at a time when home gardeners were just starting to think of sowing seed.

Biodynamic gardening techniques were worked out in Austria in the twenties by Rudolf Steiner, who made a connection between the use of the new synthetic chemical fertilizers and a decline in crop yields and vegetable nutritive values. Steiner recommended a holistic approach to agriculture and gardening based on returning organic material to the soil. He looked closely at the growing environment of each plant, particularly a plant's relationship with neighboring plants. Companion planting, he thought, could enhance plants' growth rates if the correct plants were juxtaposed. Insects could be lured away from crops or repelled by companions.

Gardeners interested in intensive gardening will find the following books rewarding reading:

Koepf, H. *Bio-Dynamic Agriculture, An Introduction*, Spring Valley, N.Y.; Anthroposophic Press, 1956.

Mittleider, J. *More Food from Your Garden*, Santa Barbara, Calif.; Woodbridge Press, 1975.

Jeavons, John. *How to Grow More Vegetables Than You Ever Thought Possible on Less Land Than You Can Imagine*, rev. ed., Berkeley, Calif.; Ten Speed Press, 1979.

In the thirties and forties these two methods were combined into the Biodynamic/French Intensive system by Englishman Alan Chadwick, who taught horticulture at the University of California. The most readable exponent of the Biodynamic/French Intensive way of gardening today is John Jeavons, whose ebullient book, *How to Grow More Vegetables Than You Ever Thought Possible on Less Land Than You Can Imagine*, has been tremendously popular. Jeavons has now started a mail-order seed house, Bountiful Gardens, and sells a line of organically grown nonhybrid seeds from Chase Organic in Surrey, England.

This style of gardening focuses on deep double-dug beds layered with manure and compost, companion planting, crop rotation, and careful planning based on cultivar needs; the results are very large vegetable yields in small spaces.

Chinese Intensive Gardening. Equally interesting is the traditional and ancient Chinese Intensive style of gardening. One of the best texts, though very simple, and full of extraordinary photographs of a truly beautiful vegetable garden, is Peter Chan's *Better Vegetable Gardens the Chinese Way: Peter Chan's Raised-Bed System*. Chan is in charge of the experimental greenhouse at Oregon State University in Portland and sets out in his book the very effective home-garden techniques of southern China. The Chan system features permanent raised beds, or long mounds, four or five feet wide, a style of gardening common in southern China, where some of the most magnificent vegetables on the face of the earth are grown. Chan's beds are far shallower than those of the double-dug French Intensive method. He explains:

> There is another system, called the French Intensive method, that says the soil should be dug two shovels deep. You dig one shovel deep and make a kind of trench. Then, you stand in the trench and dig another shovel deep. This kind of system is hard for most people to practice. It is just too much work for the home garden. And with this system, much more material must be put into the bottom of the bed. You would be spending too much time and effort to finish even a small garden. And for most vegetables, one shovel deep will give plenty of room for the roots. There are some root crops like the Japanese radish, the long white one, where the roots go down almost two feet deep. So if you have some special crop, you can maybe do a small space this way. We have found that turning the soil one shovel deep is enough, because the earth below is not concrete and the roots can still go down if they want to.

Raised Beds

Raised beds are beds of improved loamy soil raised six inches to three feet above the surface of the ground. Many gardeners like the tidy look of timber- or stone-enclosed beds and find the edges of the walls comfortable to sit on while they weed and cultivate. Yet enclosures will harbor slugs, earwigs, and other disagreeable hungry mouths. Beds with sloping sides left exposed to the air, as in the Chan method, are better aerated and insect-free. Moreover, the soil in raised beds drains well and warms up earlier in springtime.

Wide Rows

Wide rows are broad beds up to five feet in width; the gardener's arm should be able to reach all the weeds from either of the sides. Wide rows are a more efficient use of space than narrow ones, and plants are usually set out in diagonal rows or a diamond pattern in order to use every bit of room.

Vertical Gardening

Vertical gardening is another space-saving technique that gets the plants off the ground and onto all sorts of plant supports—arches, arbors, poles, trellises, stakes, strings, wires, and cages. Vines and sprawlers such as lima beans, grapevines, cucumbers, melons, peas, tomatoes, and other plants whose supine habits take up valuable growing space are natural candidates for vertical gardening.

Container Gardening

Urbanites growing vegetables in pots and boxes on a city balcony seemed ridiculous a few years ago. Surprise! This difficult kind of gardening has a large number of serious practitioners who grow some very choice fruits and vegetables among the television aerials, water tanks, and smog. Nearly anything that will hold soils and plants is used—redwood tubs, old barrels, bathtubs, clay flowerpots, window boxes. For any garden vegetable the smallest container must have the capacity to hold several cubic feet of the best loam. Even suburban gardeners and country people have discovered the convenience of potted herbs or a cherry tomato or a bearing fig on the patio or inside the house.

Sheet-Plastic Gardening

Plastics have become as ubiquitous in gardening as in the rest of our lives. Sheet plastic has so many uses for the gardener that it's difficult to count them all.

In garden plots of the north, clear plastic sheeting is laid directly on the soil for a week or ten days in the spring to warm up the soil rapidly. Alaskans actually grow short-season sweet corn set in slits in sheet plastic, because this is the only way they can get the soil warm enough to produce a crop.

Black or green plastic is punched with holes and laid in rows, and seedlings are set in the soil through the holes. The plastic acts as a mulch and helps retain moisture and heat, and no weeds grow. Melons and squash do very well in the company of black plastic. The disadvantages are that it is extremely ugly and it keeps soil temperatures high—too high—for many plants. It is especially useful in first-time gardens where there is the problem of witchgrass.

Reinforced heavy sheet plastic stapled over a timber framework is used for inexpensive greenhouses, and this writer has seen, in the high mountains of Colorado at nearly ten thousand feet elevation, an entire garden growing under a pole frame tent covered with heavy plastic.

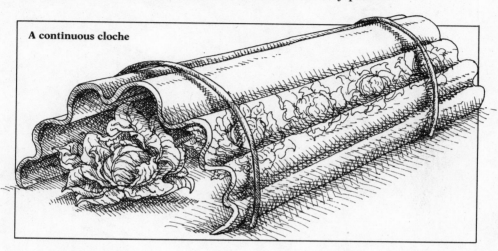

A continuous cloche

Plastic tunnels up to fifty feet long are used in home gardens as well as by commercial growers to make a warm, sheltered environment for spring and autumn crops. The tunnel forms a kind of continuous plastic cloche, but once in place, it is almost impossible to get at the plants incarcerated inside unless you roll up the sides of the tunnel. Many gardeners will find this a nuisance.

Glass Cloches

Invented by the French, perfected by the English, and little used in this country, cloches today are heavy wire frames that can be fitted with sheets of glass to make miniature greenhouses. In England these barn-shaped glass houses are lined up to make long rows and are sometimes fitted with second-story "elevators" as the plants grow.

Cloches have considerable advantages over plastic, in that they last forever, are easily moveable, and allow the gardener instant access to the plants. They also let in more sunlight, for moisture runs off the sloping glass sides more readily than it does off plastic, where condensation beads and

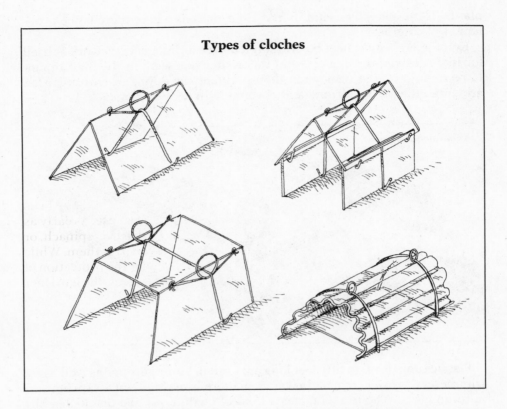

Types of cloches

films the inside surface. Cloches are quite handsome, and breakage rates are less than 2 percent a year, according to studies in England. The cloche is truly the gourmet gardener's companion, for using one it is possible to grow vegetables well into winter and in very early spring. The size of the cloche available here is twenty-four inches long, twenty-two inches wide, and nineteen inches high, though abroad many different sizes and several shapes are available.

Cloche gardening deserves a book to itself, but the only one I know of is *Gardening with Cloches*, an out-of-print English book by Louis N. Flawn. The English use cloches in complicated shifts and series all year round. The general approach is to set one part of the garden aside for cloche growing. Off-season crops from late fall through early spring are the focus of concentration, and many of the cultivars grown are winter types specially bred to take cold temperatures. Winter lettuces in particular are favored, and these make a very choice midwinter treat here for mid-Atlantic, Pacific Coast, and southern gardeners. Regions of heavy snowfall are obviously not the place to try cloches in winter. In spring, tomatoes, beans, melons, and cucumbers can be sown beneath the glass six weeks before the spring frosts end, or seedlings set out under glass two or three weeks before the frost-free days commence.

Two-strip cropping is a a basic cloche-gardening tactic. The section of the garden set aside for two-strip cropping must be sheltered from winds and should get good sunlight in the off-season. The soil must be brought up to superb quality.

Two parallel garden beds two feet wide and as long as you wish (or have enough glass to cover) are plotted out with a path between them. The beds are generally prepared in late summer or autumn for spring use. As early as February in England, the seed of carrots, beans, mâche, lettuce, spinach, or radishes is sown in one row and the cloches set in position over them. While these plants are growing rapidly to table perfection under the protection of the cloches, before the leaves have even appeared on the trees, the gardener starts seedlings inside, timed to coincide with the harvest of the first row of cloched plants, six to eight weeks after germination. As the first row is harvested, the new seedlings are set in the second bed, and the cloches are shifted over to that row. The first row, now empty of plants, may be planted with a cover crop or reinvigorated with compost and manure and planted again with seeds that will mature in late summer or autumn without the protection of glass.

There is only one source of the standard Chase cloches in this country at present, but if you travel to England, you can choose among many different sizes and shapes of cloche frames. On this side of the Atlantic, cloches can be bought from Walt Nicke.

The Best Cultivars

Picking the right cultivars for the gourmet garden from the shining pictures in the seed catalogs is a difficult business. There are too many qualities that take precedence over flavor. Some cultivars have been bred to suit specific climates or soils, such as winter lettuces which are able to withstand very low temperatures. Breeders are increasingly interested in developing plants with built-in resistances to diseases, and select for these resistances rather than for qualities of texture or taste. Sometimes plants are carefully developed to give a strain that has a particular growth habit or unusual shape, as globe-shaped carrots or white eggplants. Flavor may be a secondary concern in such selection. Early maturity is another trait that is hailed as great news in the catalogs. Ease of harvesting is very important with commercial growers, who want fruits that can be picked rapidly and easily, so plants may be developed that have their fruits borne sticking up in the air or at the ends of branches at the expense of superior taste. Yield is another important consideration to commercial growers—how many tons of broccoli to the acre they get makes a difference on the bottom line. Yet a choice cultivar may not be a heavy yielder and may slip away into the background because it is not. Both commercial growers and home gardeners who have root cellars are interested in the storage qualities of fruits and vegetables. An apple or carrot or scorzonera may have extraordinary flavor but be a "poor keeper" and disappear from the catalogs. Appearance—size, color, and uniformity of shape—is of major importance to commercial growers and seed houses. The big, red, shiny, luscious-looking fruit or vegetable without much taste is a far better seller than a rough-skinned, small cultivar with superb flavor. It's sad but true.

Personal taste and trial and error are the surest ways for a gardener to find the most succulent, delicious cultivars, but there are a few tricks to make picking out the tastiest types easier. Some seed houses, such as the Urban Farmer, Nichols, Le Marché, Demonchaux, and William Dam, concentrate on types and varieties that make the choicest table fare. A buyer can expect that fine taste and quality have motivated their catalog choices.

Many gardeners go through catalogs picking out the newest hybrids under the false impression that *new* and *hybrid* are synonymous with *better*. Hybrids are usually inferior in flavor to open-pollinated or pureline cultivars, though commercial growers find the hybrid uniformity in ripening dates, shapes, and sizes very convenient. Home growers want not only the best flavors but a crop that ripens over a period of weeks rather than all at once; hybrid crops tend to mature at the same time. Stay away from hybrids unless you want this feature.

Early cultivars have been selected for their quick-maturing qualities above all other aspects of fruiting, including flavor. Avoid them, if succulence and taste are your desire. Dwarf types, highly touted in catalogs and popular garden literature these days, are also a poor choice for the gourmet gardener, for they are generally short on flavor.

A very good way to find cultivars with good flavor that appeal to your taste is to order from seed companies that sell samplers, small packets of five or six cultivars from the same species. An outstanding company in this respect is the Urban Farmer, which offers its customers bundles of sample packets in nearly every seed category: four kinds of beets; eight types of runner beans; four broad bean cultivars; Swiss chard from Australia, Japan, and Denmark; four kinds of oriental cucumbers; and so on. Grow them side by side, taste-test them when they are ripe, and make a decision at table rather than a choice based on a page of shining printer's ink. Le Jardin du Gourmet also offers sample packets of most of their French imports.

It is genetic background above all other factors that gives different cultivars of fruits and vegetables sometimes strikingly unique flavors, but other factors may also affect aromas and tastes. The bouquet and flavors of garden produce can vary according to the soil. Everyone knows that wine grapes, *Vitis vinifera*, of the same type can have markedly different qualities according to the soil, slope, and sunlight of their environment. Apple flavors also show great differences from region to region and even from orchard to orchard. The French and English cider apples, with their distinctive flavors and good cider characteristics, are not the same when grown in North America and make very different ciders. Seed from the same packet grown in different soils and under different climatic conditions will taste subtly different to someone with a discerning palate.

All-American Selections (AAS) catch many gardeners' eyes in the catalogs. This organization was set up in 1932 by seed dealers to evaluate new cultivars of flowers and vegetables. Although flavor is one of the characteristics the judges look for when they make their annual selections, they also consider fruit size, disease resistance, vigor, and productivity. But the major consideration is whether the plant is adaptable to a wide range of soils and climates. General quality in several categories, rather than specific excellences, are the hallmark of AAS cultivars. These plants will grow almost anywhere in the country but are rarely outstanding in flavor.

Sampling the peas and raspberries from neighbors' gardens is a logical way of tasting different strains and cultivars. Tom Vorbeck of Chapin, Illinois, has taken a lot of the guesswork out of choosing apple cultivars. Tom runs a mail-order apple service called Applesource, which allows customers to choose from the fruits of nearly one hundred apple cultivars. The apples you choose are shipped to you in the mail. A partial listing includes Arkansas Black, Ben Davis, Black Gilliflower, Chenango Strawberry, Cox's Orange Pippin, Grimes Golden, King David, Melrose, Molly's Delicious, Ozark Gold, Pitmaston Pineapple, Roxbury Russet, Snow Apple, Summer Rambo, Turley Winesap, Winter Banana, Pearmain, Swaar, Yellow Bellflower. When was the last time you bought any of these at the supermarket? By tasting and comparing these rare, old, and unusual apples, you can decide what you would like to grow.

A delightful source of small fruits for tasting and comparing is found at the annual member's day of the New York State Fruit Testing Cooperative Association in Geneva, New York. The third Thursday of September is given over to an incredible display of plums, peaches, cherries, pears, apples, berries of all kinds, nectarines, apricots, and grapes in one of the most stunning assemblages of fruits on the continent. Many grower-members bring unusual examples of their own fruit cultivars from backyard orchards and gardens to share and swap. Quite a few of the fruits are experimental cultivars that have not been released for public sale. This is an unrivaled chance to try distinctive fruits.

Good Seedlings

Master gardeners and agricultural extension people name seed-starting difficulties as a big stumbling block for too many home gardeners. Not very many gardeners start the season with good, strong, healthy seedlings at the proper state of development for setting out in the garden. Low light, warm temperatures, and careful timing of seed sowing get the young plants going on the right root. But too many green-thumbers, impatient to hurry things along, sow seed far too early. In northern New England an old folk saying— "Start your seeds on Town Meeting Day"—has done a lot of harm over the decades. Town Meeting Day falls in early March in Vermont, nearly three months before the last frosts. With the exception of celery and a few others, seeds should not be started indoors until four to eight weeks before garden-transplant time. A poor start in the seedling flat usually means a poor plant in the garden, with less than superb fruit.

Alaskan gardeners, who start everything indoors, even sweet corn, know more about the subject of seed starting than most of us. The Alaskan extension service has boiled down seed-starting times to a science. Here are some approximate seed starting periods for the major groups of vegetables:

	Weeks Before Last Spring Frost
Squashes, cucurbits	Three to four
Celery, celeriac	Ten to twelve
Tomatoes	Seven to nine
Peppers	Six to seven
Cole crops, lettuces	Four to six

Difficult Seeds

Some seeds need to be scarified or soaked before germination stimuli can tickle the inside of the seed. Peas, spinach, beets, petunias, and morning glories all have hard coats. Sometimes seeds are scarified before they are packaged, but often the gardener has to do it at home. Sanding hard seeds with a nail file thins the coat and softens it. Beet and spinach seeds germinate better if they get the rolling-pin treatment: Put the seed in a bag or a folded cloth and run a rolling pin over them a few times. Other seeds, such as parsley, parsnip, asparagus, and okra seeds, need a good soaking overnight in warm (not hot) soapy water. Use soap, not detergent, and plant them immediately the next morning. Don't let them dry out. Special instructions for seed treatment may come with the seeds, so be sure to read any attached labels and all the packet information. One of the most useful books on seed treatment is Ann Reilly's *Park's Success with Seeds*.

Planting Mediums

Pellets, cubes, and peat pots are popular for starting seed in. Gardeners like them better than the old soil-filled flats because there is no transplanting trauma and no tedious thinning of little seedlings. However, at transplant time these pots and pellets are a root barrier for the young plant unless the outside is carefully peeled away, and this pulls at the rootlets with unavoidable damage. Healthier, strong, and undamaged seedlings can be grown in soil blocks.

To make soil blocks the gardener uses a favorite soil mix, dampened so that it will hold together, then punches out strong little blocks with a special implement called a block maker. The blocks are set in a flat and the seed sown, usually two to each block. After germination, the weaker seedlings are cut off with a small scissors. Soil block implements are available from Green River Tools.

Commercial growing mediums found in hardware stores, supermarkets, and garden supply shops are better avoided. There are no manufacturing standards for these mixes, and while some are good, others have turned out to be worse than useless. Problems have resulted from excessive amounts of heavy metals, excess salt, low pH, nutrient deficiencies, and imbalances. By mixing your own growing medium in a five-gallon plastic pail with a cover, or other clean container, you know exactly what you've got. Here are some of the best potting-mixture recipes. Do not use beach sand in these mixtures—the high salt content will kill seedlings.

Cornell University Mix
8 quarts vermiculite
8 quarts shredded peat moss
2 tablespoons superphosphate
2 tablespoons ground limestone
8 tablespoons dried cow manure or steamed bonemeal

Peter Chan's Mix
1 part soil
1 part sand or perlite
1 part peat moss
1 part manure

Brooklyn Botanic Garden Mix
4 parts soil
2 parts sand
2 parts leaf mold or peat moss
1 part dried cow manure
½ cup bonemeal for every 2½ gallons mix

The soil you use in these mixes must be pasteurized to prevent damping-off and other diseases. Pasteurizing soil is done simply by putting garden soil in a large baking pan, dampening it thoroughly (it is the permeating steam that does the job), and covering it tightly with aluminum foil or a cover. Insert a meat thermometer into the soil and bake in an oven set to 200 degrees F until the soil reaches a temperature of 160 to 170 degrees. Hold at this temperature for thirty minutes. You may need to turn the oven off at this point, for it is important that the soil temperature not go above 180 degrees. The higher heat can break down some of the soil nutrients into toxic elements. Compost that is used in a starter mix should also be pasteurized.

Microwave ovens can be used to pasteurize soil if there is a thermometer probe. Set the oven at 180 degrees and insert the probe into the foil-covered soil. Leave the pan in the oven after it shuts off at 180 degrees thirty minutes.

Thirty minutes at 140 degrees F kills most fungi and bacteria.
Thirty minutes at 160 degrees F kills soil insects.
Thirty minutes at 180 degrees F kills most weed seeds.

Germination

Large and medium-size seeds are covered over lightly or pushed well into the soil block. Fine seed, including lettuce seed, is allowed to lie on the surface. Mist or water the soil lightly after sowing and cover the flats with sheets of glass to hold the moisture in until the seeds germinate. The flats should be kept in dim light in a place where the temperature remains a steady 65 to 75 degrees F for most garden vegetables. The cole crops all germinate better in cool temperatures, around 55 degrees. Seed catalogs or the seed packets should carry specific germination requirements for different species and cultivars, but many neglect to give the gardener this important piece of information. If you have seed new to you and without packet instructions, take the trouble to check Ann Reilly's *Park's Success with Seeds*, or a gardening textbook such as Clyde L. Calvin and Donald M. Knutson's *Modern Home Gardening*.

Soil-heating cable laid under the flats is an excellent way of providing gentle, even heat both night and day. If you have a small flat or two of seeds to start, the top of the refrigerator is usually a cozy place. As soon as the seedlings are up, remove the glass covers and shift the flats to a sunny location or under a grow-light with a fresh fluorescent tube. Old tubes emit weak light waves that don't do the seedlings much good.

Temperature fluctuations inside the house between night and day can throw the seedlings into a decline. Optimum daytime temperatures for most vegetable plants range between 70 and 78 degrees F with nighttime temperatures about 10 degrees cooler. Cole crops like daytime highs around 65 degrees and nights down to around 55 degrees. Misting or use of a room humidifier keeps seedlings healthier. This is especially important in rooms that are heated by wood stoves; the air can become very dry. The planting medium should be allowed to nearly dry out between waterings.

Hardening Off

A transition period of about two weeks prepares the seedlings for life in the great outdoors. It is vital that they adjust gradually to wind, direct sunlight, and highly variable temperature fluctuations. The first few days outside, the plants must be sheltered, and a cold frame or wind-protected patio are logical places to put them. They should get sun in gradually increasing doses.

Cold frames are fine places to harden off young plants, for the covers can be closed at night and opened just a crack on chill, windy days. There are solar-activated devices, sold under the trade name Solarvent, that automatically open the cold frame cover when interior temperatures reach 75 degrees F and close it when they drop to 68 degrees. This gizmo can save your seedlings from cooking. Many home gardeners have had the wretched experience of losing several hundred thriving young seedlings in a few sunny hours because they forgot to open the cold frame cover.

Transplanting to the Garden

Setting the seedlings out into their permanent home is best done on an overcast, windless day in the late afternoon. It is even better if you can finish the job just before a rain.

Tomato plants should be set in place after the stakes to support them are driven in. Lay them horizontally with their crowns facing away from the direction of the prevailing wind; the section of stem that is in contact with the soil will put down feeding roots that also serve to anchor the plant securely. Tomato cage supports are put in place after the plants are set out.

As you transplant, give each young plant a cup or so of starter solution. This can be a mild manure tea or one tablespoon of a high-phosphorus fertilizer (10-52-17 or similar analysis) dissolved in a gallon of water. There are many kickoff fertilizer mixes available, from soluble seaweed powder to special formulas for tomatoes or the *Brassicae*.

Direct Seeding

Most vegetable seeds are sown directly in the garden in beds of warm, fine soil. The smaller the soil particles, the greater the contact they have with liberating moisture. Soil can be warmed up in seven to ten days during a cold spring by laying sheets of clear plastic over beds that were prepared in autumn. Seeds double their germination rates when a 50-degree soil is raised to 60 degrees F.

Instead of raking soil over the seeds, sprinkle them with fine compost or a mixture of soil and sphagnum moss. Soil can crust over and make seedling emergence difficult or impossible. Some slow seeds can be sown with the lusty radishes, which emerge first and break any soil crust. Crusted-over soil, more often than defective seed, is responsible for scanty seedling numbers.

Fluid Sowing

The British National Vegetable Research Station came up several years ago with a germination and planting technique that allowed gardeners to force sprouts indoors, then sow the already germinated seeds in a gelatin-like medium directly in the garden. Seedling emergence rates were considerably higher than with standard dry seeding.

The extension service at Cornell University has worked out a homemade fluid-gel system. Seeds are presprouted on a paper plate covered with damp paper towels and kept in a warm place, such as the top of the refrigerator or the hot-water heater. A few days after the seeds germinate, they are transferred to the fluid gel. This gel may be made by cooking about three level tablespoons of cornstarch in two cups of water. The mixture should be the consistency of shampoo in a tube. The cooled gel is poured into a sandwich-size plastic bag; then the sprouts are added and gently stirred in until they are evenly distributed in the mixture. The bag is tied at the top and carried out to the garden, where the prepared soil bed awaits seeds. At the planting site, the gardener cuts a tiny corner off the bag, large enough to allow a sprout free passage. The sprout-laden gel is squirted along in the furrows of the bed, then lightly covered with sieved soil and watered to help the rootlets make contact with the soil particles.

This technique is particularly helpful with the slow, low-germination plants, such as parsley, carrots, and parsnips, and with small, hard-to-handle seed. Peas, beans, and other large seeds don't need fluid-gel sowing. However, these big boys will do startlingly well when a culture of nitrogen-fixing bacteria is added to the soil as they are sown. A number of seed houses sell this culture under the trade name Legume-Aid. It is especially efficacious in new ground that hasn't been gardened before. It is sprinkled in the furrow before the seeds are planted, and covered over as soon as possible, for light destroys the helpful bacteria.

Water

Watering has been called the most misunderstood aspect of gardening. The seedlings may be models of vigor and health, the soil rich and fine, but unless an adequate and regular supply of water gets to the plants throughout the growing season, the quantity and quality of the fruits will be seriously damaged. Not many vegetable gardens get what they really need for water. Water stress symptoms that show up are tough, woody texture; bitterness; early flower and fruit drop; and small, misshapen fruits. Tomatoes suffer blossom-end rot. Such harvests are hardly a cook's delight.

Rutgers University researchers discovered that some plants have critical periods in their development during which good supplies of water are absolutely vital if the plant is to fruit successfully. Sweet corn needs abundant water at the stage where it tassels out and makes silk; cucumbers, melons, green beans, and tomatoes need it from the blossoming stage through the fruiting stage. Potatoes must have good water supplies when they reach the point of setting tubers, and peppers demand it from seedling age through maturity. Lettuce, broccoli, cabbage, and cauliflower have their most crucial period of water demand during head development. For maximum flavor and quality, all vegetable plants must get the water and nutrients they need without stress.

For the gourmet gardener, the dryland garden, a garden which is not watered because the gardener trusts in the weather to supply rainfall regularly through the growing season, is a bad risk. Watering cans and squirting hoses are the most inefficient and inadequate ways to water a garden. Still, the hose can help if perforated coffee cans have been sunk in the ground beside each plant when the seedlings were set out. By filling the cans with water once a week and mulching around the plant, a steady, even supply of water gets to the roots. A disadvantage is that the soil around the root zone may become too warm, and mosquitoes will find the breeding habitat congenial.

Watering cans are not much good, no matter how handsome they are, unless the garden is very small and the gardener checks to see if the soil-wetting front has reached down to the hungry roots.

Sprinklers

Sprinkler systems have been enormously improved in the past few years. Now they can be programmed to apportion heavy or light amounts of water to certain sections of the garden according to the needs of the plants that grow there. Automatic timers wet down one area in the garden weekly, and another area every two or three days. Digital timers allow a sprinkler to run for a few minutes, then shut off to let the soil absorb the water before it switches back on, avoiding puddling and surface runoff. Sprinklers can be programmed to run at specific times of day, such as early morning and evening, when evaporation rates are lower.

But wind flow can disturb a sprinkler pattern, and the systems use as much as 70 percent more water than a trickle irrigation setup. Sprinklered gardens also mean that the owner stays out while the sprinkling is going on. Arid regions of the country where water supplies are limited may prohibit sprinkler systems.

Smith and Hawken carry Gardena modular watering sprinkler systems; they are of high quality and have thoughtfully designed components that allow a gardener to arrange a sprinkler layout tailored to his or her particular garden shape and vegetable needs.

Trickle Irrigation

Trickle, or drip, irrigation was developed in Israel's desert gardens almost half a century ago, but it has just hit this country's home gardens.

Experts say it is the watering system of our near future. There is no more efficient and conservative way of using water in the garden. Trickle irrigation provides a low, steady volume of water directly to a plant's root zone a drop at a time. There are four types of emitters. *Twin-wall* emitters are built like a hose inside a hose. Water fills the inner hose full, then moves out through the inner walls to fill up the outer hose. Here it oozes through tiny holes spaced a foot or so apart, and slowly saturates the soil. *Biwall* emitters consist of a hose with a smaller perforated hose attached along one side. When the water pressure is equalized in the main hose, it moves into the smaller hose and emits a drop from each perforation. *Soaker* hose simply oozes its entire length instead of at strategic points. *Point* emitters are like branches off the main hose, and the terminal points supply moisture to isolated plants.

In California and the Southwest, trickle-irrigation components of many designs, types, and brand names can be bought in supermarket-like garden supply stores. Easterners will find components and packaged systems increasingly easier to find both in garden shops and through mail order.

The advantages of a drip irrigation system outweigh the problems, which include the initial expense and the possible clogging of the tiny emitter holes with mineral deposits, algae growth, or even soil particles. Mice and other rodents have been caught gnawing at trickle-irrigation components in some parts of the country. Aside from the savings in water (of growing concern to gardeners), trickle systems let the gardener work among the plants at any time, and water gets only to the roots. Black plastic mulch is often used with a drip system.

WATER WARNING

Do not water cantaloupes or other hand melons as they begin to ripen. Onions should not be watered once their leaves bend over when they are mature.

How much water a garden needs depends on the soil type, the crops growing in it, rainfall, wind, transpiration rates, and the amount and intensity of sunlight. It is an old garden rule of thumb that an inch of water per week is a good average.

More precisely, the wetting front should move down through the soil to a depth of two feet minimum at each watering. (Water seeps slowly down through the soil in horizontal layers. When one layer is soaked through, the moisture then seeps down to the next stratum. The saturated layer is called the wetting front.) Obviously one cannot dig a hole each time the garden is watered to see if the moisture has made it down to the two-foot level. Instead, it is possible to estimate the amount given in one way or another.

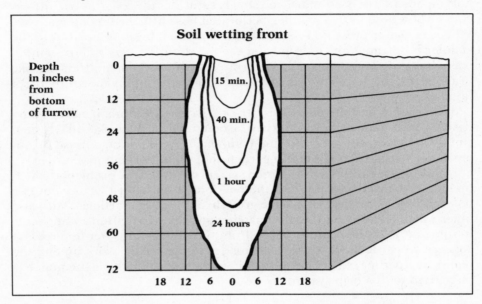

Soil wetting front

Depth in inches from bottom of furrow

0
12
24
36
48
60
72

15 min.
40 min.
1 hour
24 hours

18 12 6 0 6 12 18

If you are using a sprinkler system, place several cans in the sprinkler pattern area. Note the time the water was turned on. At the end of the watering period, measure the water level in the cans and take the average as the depth of available water that was applied. Use the chart below to figure how deeply the wetting front extends. For example, if your soil is a fine sandy loam that is very dry, and you wish to be sure there is moisture 24 inches down in the soil, run the sprinkler until 3.8 inches of water collect in your measuring can.

Another way is to measure the amount of water that flows through your hose at a given force in a given time. With water at standard household pressure of 40 psi, a ⅝-inch garden hose that is fifty feet long has a flow rate of 6.4 gallons per minute. To give a fifty-by-twenty-foot garden (one thousand square feet) an inch of water will take 620 gallons of water and about one and a half hours.

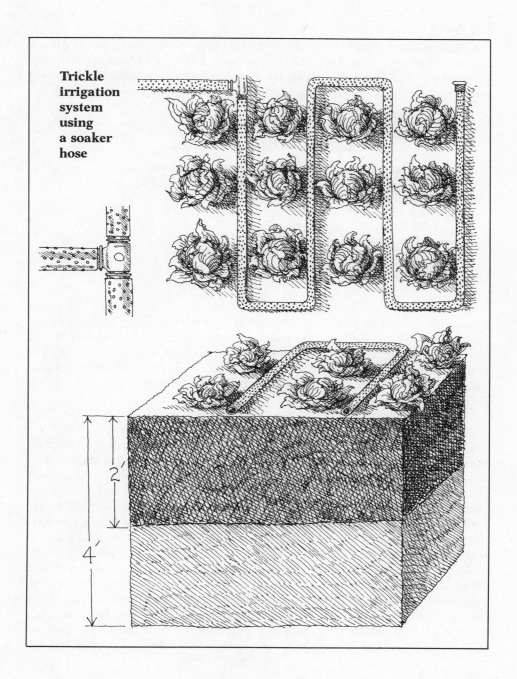

Trickle irrigation system using a soaker hose

2'

4'

Different garden soils have different water-holding capacities. If plants have reached the point of wilt, the following amounts of water are necessary for each foot of soil depth to bring the water level back to capacity. To bring a depth of two feet of soil back to capacity takes quite a lot of water.

Soil Water-Holding Capacities

Soil type	Inches of available water per foot of soil depth
Coarse sand	0.5
Very fine sandy loam	1.9
Silt loam	2.6
Clay	2.8

From Clyde L. Calvin and Donald M. Knutson, *Modern Home Gardening* (New York: John Wiley & Sons, 1983), p. 236.

Country gardeners often think they have hit upon a marvelous way to get more mileage out of their water by using gray water on the garden. Laundry-waste water should not be put on vegetable plants (or other plants), because most detergents contain boron and chlorine. The chlorine will kill your plants, and the boron can build up to toxic levels. Bathwater can be used in a pinch, but generally the gray stuff contains pathogens that may be dangerous to human health.

Mulch

One of the best tricks in the gardener's bag is the use of mulches. A mulch is any material laid on the soil to hold back weed growth and to reduce soil-moisture evaporation. Organic mulches are most valuable because they will break down over the season and can be mixed into the soil to improve and enrich it. Salt hay, straw, spoiled hay, leaves, used hops, buckwheat hulls, cocoa bean hulls, and peat moss are organic mulches favored by gardeners. Hortpaper is a thirty-two-inch-wide biodegradable mulch made of peat moss and recycled paper. It can be tilled into the soil at the end of the season. Salt hay is one of the best mulches of all because it is seed-free and clean and doesn't mat down. A bale of it can put a thin layer over a fifty-by-twenty-foot (one-thousand-square-foot) garden. Straw, the stalk remainder of cereal crops, is another excellent mulch, but as it breaks down, it takes nitrogen out of the soil. Spoiled hay, especially if it is clover or vetch or another legume hay, will add nitrogen to the soil as it breaks down, but the seed will also give you a lusty crop just where you don't want it. Spoiled hay is not a good mulch to use around lettuces; the musty odor taints the lettuces' outer leaves. Wood chips, sawdust, and, in the South, gin trash, have all been used for garden mulches, but these have distinct disadvantages. The chips and sawdust can be very acidic, and they take nitrogen from the soil as they break down over time. Arsenicals are used on cotton crops, so gin trash may contain this dangerous element as well as weed seed. Compost is a clean, even a noble, mulch. It is rich, nutrient-laden humus that builds and conditions the soil as it sinks in, free of weed seeds and diseases. It is an ideal mulch, but rarely is there enough of it to do an entire garden.

Gardeners using organic mulches for the first time tend to lay it down much too early. Mulches should not be put down in the garden until the soil is warmed up to a minimum of 60 degrees F. Before laying down mulch, the garden should be weeded and well watered. Wait until young transplants have gotten a good roothold on the soil before mulching them.

A thick bed of mulch six inches deep will flatten out to three inches in a few weeks, and that's acceptable. It will do what you want it to. As the season goes on and the mulch breaks down into the soil, you may pile on more.

AND, AT LAST, HARVESTING

Harvest the garden vegetables as they reach maturity for the finest flavors. Don't let vegetables stand until they become woody and coarse. Picking them too young can result in disappointing flavor, too. Immature vegetables taste disagreeable. But if you have chosen fine cultivars and given them good soil, sufficient water, and nutrients, and have encouraged rapid, even growth to the point of early maturity, these marvelous things will have reached the acme of perfection. The textures will be crisp or creamy or firm and meaty; the flavors and aromatic oils full-bodied. These are the basis for extraordinary dishes.

Tools and Gadgets

The cheap, stamped-metal tools that were all a gardener could find a few years ago have competition. Imported English and French forged tools of high quality and polished aluminum hand tools, aesthetically pleasing and good to work with, have re-established the gardener's pride and pleasure in the work of growing plants. Smith and Hawken's fine line of Bulldog Tools are beautiful, high-grade implements, and include such desirable items as the Irish garden spade, a tilthing fork for breaking up compacted soils, and the Stalham (or Swan) drawing hoe. The same fine tools have been scaled down to children's sizes, and several are specially adapted for disabled gardeners. Smith and Hawken also carry Haws watering cans and the Rolls-Royce of watering systems, Gardena sprinklers, with all the associated gadgets.

Spades, hoes and shovels, all should be cleaned after each use, and they should be sharpened regularly with a 10-inch bastard file. The difference a minute's sharpening makes in the performance of a tool is impressive. It's an easy, quick job.

Hoe blades have only one bevel, but the angle varies from 45 to 85 degrees to the flat of the blade. The 85-degree angle is for general hoeing work, and it holds its sharpness rather well. The acute 45-degree angle will need frequent honing; it gives a sharp cutting action. As you sharpen, try to keep to the original angle. Deliberate, accurate strokes all at the same angle give superior results. When the blade is sharpened, turn the hoe over, and with a few light strokes, holding the file flat against the blade, remove the wire edge the sharpening procedure created.

Shovels and spades have the bevel edge on the inside surface of the blade. Be sure all the soil and mud is cleaned off before putting the file to the metal.

Cordless Phone

The cordless phone is a tremendous aid for gardeners. How many times have you heard the faint, faraway ringing and ringing of the phone and sprinted from the garden, kicking up clods of dirt as you leaped for the instrument only to find the caller gave up a millisecond before your hand grasped the receiver? The cordless phone hitches onto your belt or goes into a garden basket. You can answer the apparatus and carry on conversations while you're weeding the onions or checking the lettuces for slugs. Find cordless phones at electronics stores and wherever phone equipment is sold in your area. Nurserymen and horticulturists all over the country use these handy gadgets to stay in touch with the world and still get the garden work done.

Home Computer

The home computer can be enormously helpful to gardeners. Use it to store information on seed orders, nursery stock, crop rotations, cross-pollination requirements, vegetable and fruit harvest yields, the addresses of botanical gardens, seed companies, soil test results, and so on. If you have graphics programs and software, you can map out your garden plan and work up landscape designs, drawing in pathways and fences. The computer is ideal for keeping good garden records year after year, and this information can be a great help in planning and ordering for next year's garden.

Rototiller

The rototiller is an odd machine. Gardeners either like 'em or they leave 'em. They are a lot of help in working up fresh ground and fining a rough soil, and almost indispensable in tilling in green-manure crops. However, they should not be used as cultivators to keep weeds down, for frequent use of a tiller in the garden allows the tines to beat the soil at the bottom of each stroke and make a denser layer of soil there. Frequent tiller use also destroys the aggregate soil clumps and reduces the soil's water-holding ability.

Rototillers are far easier to use on level ground than on a hillside or terraced garden, where they are awkward, unstable, and dangerous. A strong, experienced gardener, not afraid of hard work and armed with a sharpened spade, a shovel, and a garden fork can do a better job at preparing small soil beds and gardens than any rototiller in existence. The tiller makes the job easier and faster, but not necessarily better. Gardeners who want double-dug or deeply worked beds will only use a tiller for green-manuring.

Chipper-Shredder

For rural gardeners and landowners, the chipper-shredder that runs off a tractor PTO or that has its own gasoline engine is worth its weight in *fraisesdes bois*. These noisy but useful machines gobble up old cornstalks, tomato vines, pruned branches and twigs, deadwood, pea vines, cabbage stalks, brush, and brambles, and spit out shredded mulch or small material for fast composting. The brush heaps and that pile of old tree branches and stalks disappear in a few minutes.

Removable-Side Wheelbarrow

Heaven knows why these wonderful barrows faded from the gardening scene to be replaced by the plywood and cheap metal garden cart. A well-built wheelbarrow will carry heavy loads without complaining or collapsing with bent axles. The removable-side barrow can accommodate awkward objects, such as fenceposts, cordwood, enormous daikon radishes, a great big pumpkin, or a load of lime or branches and stalks. Although barrows are easier to tip over than a garden cart, they are more useful in the garden because they fit into tighter spaces and are highly maneuverable in snug corners.

Every gardener has certain items he or she considers indispensable—special tool hangers, a scuffle hoe, a pair of wooden gardening clogs from Belgium. Here are some good ones.

Kneeling Pad

Some gardeners like strap-on knee pads, but they pinch the backs of your legs and are uncomfortable in hot weather. More versatile is the thick sponge-foam kneeling pad. (It is very useful for canoeing, too.) It's washable, and you can kneel or sit on it.

Headnet

Blackflies are the most pernicious of insects. They arrive at seed-sowing time, followed closely by the orange-eyed deerfly. Both swarm and whine around a gardener's head with a spiteful persistence that has driven many erstwhile gardeners straight to the screened-in porch and a good novel. There are several preparations of repellent on the market now that contain 90 to 100 percent diethyltoluamide, the most effective repellent against blackflies and mosquitoes. But in heavily infested areas nothing works as well as a headnet. It is not unusual in northern New England to see gardeners done up in mesh headnets as they seed and transplant. Sporting-goods stores and fishing-tackle shops carry them.

Baskets, Trugs, and Aluminum Bushel Containers

Gardeners have a passion for baskets, from the shallow, dainty things built to carry a few lilies and roses to strong ash and split hickory apple baskets that can take heavy loads (a bushel of apples weighs about forty five pounds), knock around for years, and still look beautiful. Many garden sheds hold fine collections of baskets. Choose what you like, but examine the handles carefully before you buy. Handle materials should support the weight of the basket across the bottom. Cheap baskets have flimsy handles that soon pull out.

The English trug is a sturdy, oblong, shallow split basket with feet and a handle that supports the bottom. It will carry a load of pears or several quarts of berries and other odds and ends.

The galvanized heavy metal bushel basket with rope handles is enormously useful to gardeners. It can be lugged through the beds and filled with weeds, dead flowers, broken stalks, and stuff intended for the compost heap. It can be filled with squash or apples or potatoes. It holds the sand as you work on your brick garden walk. It lasts forever and is indestructible.

Goatskin Garden Gloves

These supple pearl-gray gloves are tough and snug. They stretch and conform to the gardener's hand and are fine enough to allow delicate work. The natural lanolin in the leather keeps your hands from getting rough and dried-out through contact with the soil. Goatskin gloves are *the* gardening gloves.

Dibble

The dibble, like the bulb-setter, is a simple and very useful hand tool. You plunge it into the ground and work it about a bit when transplanting or use it to draw seed drills in prepared beds.

Shade Cloths

Very useful for growing celery or radishes in summer heat or for starting seedlings in midsummer, shade cloths are made of a light-weight, strong polypropylene mesh that comes in several densities: 53 percent shade for tropical plants and flowering cactus, 60 percent shade for general plant growth, and 73 percent for plants at rest or ones that are being acclimated to the shift indoors in the autumn. Shade cloths can be bought from Mellingers.

Bird Mesh

If you grow any fruits at all, you will soon find that the birds try to pick everything you've got. Sometimes these avian gourmets will strip your elderberry, currant, raspberry, and blackberry bushes before the fruit is even ripe. Plastic webbing is not the complete answer, for the birds can get at the fruit through the large mesh openings, and the plant sends up branches and leaves through the holes, making it the very devil to get the webbing off again. Nylon mesh, as fine as you can get it, is the material. Many garden supply houses carry it.

Garden Bench

Every garden needs a bench at the end of it where the pear tree grows. The bench is to the gardener what the rail fence used to be to the farmer. There you can look over your smallholding, mark vegetable progress, solve problems, and lay plans for next year in the garden.

THE CLASSIC GREEN SALAD

The green leafy plants that make up the classic green salad are tremendously diverse—hundreds of lettuces, the chicories and endives, spinaches, chard, orache, greens, fennel, cresses, corn salad, purslane, rape, sorrel, and dozens more. Gardening cooks who wish to explore the delights of the green salad bowl will find useful information in the following books:

Larkcom, Joy, *The Salad Garden*. New York: Viking, 1984.
Proulx, E. Annie, *The Fine Art of Salad Gardening*. Emmaus, Pa.: Rodale Press, 1985.

CHAPTER 2

THE MAGNIFICENT CRUDITÉS

BRASSICAE: Cauliflower / Flowering
Kale / Kohlrabi / Bunching Onions
Carrot / Celeriac / Celery / Cucumber
Radish / Rat-tailed Radish / Turnip

At the turn of the century Gertrude Jeckyll taught English gardeners to treat the garden as a canvas and perennials as a palette of infinitely varied colors. There are parallels in vegetable gardening and fine cuisine. The gardeners and cooks of Provence have developed extraordinary arrangements using a mélange of raw vegetables called *crudités*, so skillfully arranged that this too, can be considered an art form. In this country, caterers and cooks have made crudités the complex and beautiful focal point of elaborate summer entertainments, masterly collages of fruits and vegetables in grand dimensions. Martha Stewart is the food and entertainment editor for *House Beautiful* and a professional caterer who excels in crudités arrangements. She grows many of the vegetables she uses in her displays in the family garden. Stewart writes in her book *Entertaining*:

I . . . love the medium of the crudités. The color, texture, shape, and taste of fresh vegetables are remarkable. . . . Of course, there is a world of difference between a careless and a careful presentation of crudités. Crudités are ... closer to a good still life, an artful edible exhibit. Crudités have indeed become an art form among food professionals, so much so that each good caterer in New York is known for his particular way of arranging and serving them. Crudités change with each season, too. The look of ... spring ... based on asparagus, peas and pea pods, and tiny young string beans is very different from that of late summer, when you find cherry tomatoes, orange plum tomatoes, and a rainbow of lush, bright, and full-bodied squashes.

Vegetables grown for crudités must be outstanding in flavor and texture, and handsome in color and form. Only the best is good enough. The gourmet gardener will eagerly seek through the seed catalogs to discover not only the most delicious cultivars but those with curious histories and unusual shapes and colors: round carrots, flowering kales in cream and rose, tiny bright yellow tomatoes with a piquant taste, a rainbow of radishes from snowy white to French golden to fire engine red to black Spanish types.

Carefully chosen vegetables can be transformed into artful designs as small as a little bowl of vegetables for a solitary meal or as large as a twenty-foot-long table heaped in cascades and waterfalls of grapes, nuts, cherries, melons, apples—all the produce of the garden, orchard, and nut grove. Adding branches and sprigs of fresh herbs, the leaves pinched to release the oils, will give crudités an elusive and delicious perfume.

Not all vegetables are useful in the crudités arrangement. Lettuces wilt rapidly unless the stem ends are wrapped in little plastic bags of damp vermiculite. Beets are dull and unlovely unless they are cooked and peeled, and then they bleed all over everything. Eggplants are beautiful as long as they remain whole and play a purely decorative role. Raw potatoes are neither decorative nor edible.

Many raw vegetables can be cut into curls, twists, fringes, asymmetrical chunks, coils, fans, roses, and other fanciful shapes. Cabbages, lettuces, and some squashes and fruits can be hollowed out for dips or other contrasting crudités fillings.

Vegetables that are good subjects for the garnisher's knife include celeriac, turnips, summer squashes, peppers, cucumbers, radishes, scallions, and carrots.

Witloof chicory and some of the fancy lettuces such as Prize Head with its pink and bronze outer leaves and cream-colored heart, or the spectacular red Salad Bowl, or the very beautiful German *Sprenkel* lettuce with its frilly green leaves dotted with brown speckles, deserve the extra care such wilt-prone leafage demands.

Some vegetables need to be briefly blanched in order to hold their color and fresh flavor. Cauliflower, carrots, green beans, snow peas, asparagus, broccoli, and brussels sprouts are among the vegetables that become more beautiful after a fast dip in boiling water. Vegetables should be blanched and then chilled two to three hours before they are arranged, but should not stand overnight in the refrigerator, for they lose flavor, vitamins, and luster.

RESOURCES FOR THE NOVICE GARNISHER

Garnishing and cutting vegetables into interesting and tempting shapes is an important skill for the crudités arranger. Following are several books useful to the gardener cook:

Stewart, Martha. *Entertaining*. New York: Clarkson W. Potter, Inc., 1982.
Pépin, Jacques. *La Technique*. New York: Times Books, 1976.
Haydock, Yukiko. *Japanese Garnishes*. New York: Holt, Rinehart and Winston, 1980.

Crudités can be arranged in baskets, on platters, weathered planks, picnic tables, linen cloths, dainty plates, earthenware, grass cloth, tatami mats—indeed, on whatever is harmonious with the raw material, the surroundings, and your personal taste.

The gardener cook who entertains may wish to grow a special collection of vegetables for crudités arrangements. The best of the bunch are the cole crops (flowering kale, cabbage, broccoli, cauliflower), celery, celeriac, turnips, summer squashes including zucchini and pattypan, peppers (sweet bell peppers and perhaps a variety of the hot chiles in many colors and shapes), cucumbers, radishes, the small onions, chicory, endive and lettuces, tomatoes, green beans, edible pea pods, and asparagus. Inventive gardeners will add many more types of choice vegetable delicacies.

The *Brassicae* are a maddening group, horticulturally complex and extremely diverse, embracing more than forty species, most of them subdivided into many cultivars and strains. For example, the *Oleracea*, or cabbage species, are further broken down into groups: *Acephala* includes nine kales, collards, colewort, borecole, and others; *Alboglabra* is the Chinese kale; *Botrytis* the broccolis and cauliflower; *Captitata* the many cabbages; *Gongylodes* the curious kohlrabi; *Italica* the Italian broccoli and asparagus broccoli; *Tronchuda* the Tronchuda cabbage and Portuguese kales. Almost all of these are striking and beautiful in table arrangements. Hollowed-out cabbage heads holding piquant sauces, florets of broccoli and cauliflower in bunches and heaps, the crinkled leaves of savoy cabbages and the frilly pastels of the flowering kales are all enjoyable to work with and breathtaking in effect.

CAULIFLOWER

(B. oleracea, Botrytis group)

Cauliflower, with its pure and saintly white florets, is really a thick, malformed flower cluster packed into a dense corymb. The undulating surface of the whole head looks like a miniature hilly landscape under snow. Few vegetables are so beautiful, and so amusing to arrange.

Botanically cauliflower is classed with broccoli, though it is more tender to frost, more delicate in flavor, and a greater challenge to the gardener who wants to grow perfect heads.

Cauliflower has seniority; it was known long before the more pedestrian broccoli. The Latin name, *cauliflora*, was mangled into "cole-florie" by Gerard, "cole flower" by Parkinson, and "culiflower" in Winthrop's seed list of 1635, but these spelling diversities are as nothing compared to the crimes against cauliflower that have been committed in the American kitchen, where the firm heads have been reduced to sodden, overboiled mush. Cauliflower is at its best steamed briefly until tender-crisp, and it is agreeably crunchy when raw.

There are indications that cauliflower was the queen of the *Brassicae* in former days, for Parkinson says it is more pleasing in taste than cabbage, and of "more regard and respect at good mens tables." The two ounces of "culiflower" seeds that Winthrop brought from London to Massachusetts were the most expensive of the fifty-nine plants and herbs on the bill—two shillings sixpence an ounce. William Rhind says, in his great tome on the vegetable kingdom, that cauliflower was still a rarity in England at the beginning of the seventeenth century, and only appeared "at the tables of the most opulent." He cites the incredible price of three shillings for only two cauliflower heads in 1619. England, he goes on, was a leading grower of cauliflower after the Civil War of 1688 (which Rhind calls "intestine troubles") and until the French Revolution, when all of France, Holland, and Germany clamored for English cauliflower. The climate of England is excellently suited to cauliflower production, being cool, moist, and mild. Rhind finds he must agree with Dr. Johnson, although it obviously pains him to quote the learned doctor, "whose most trivial and perhaps sometimes absurd remarks have been considered worthy of record," and he repeats Johnson's arch comment on the plant: "Of all flowers I like the cauliflower the best."

Vilmorin-Andrieux, the nineteenth-century French vegetable authority, lists seventeen cauliflower cultivars, including the Purple Cape from Sicily, several self-blanching types whose leaves enfold the entire head, and some distinctly green-headed types. There is the usual confusion in their list about what is cauliflower and what is broccoli. Waverly Root points out in *Food* that regional cauliflowers are still found in Europe—the white in Milan, a green type in Rome, purple-headed cauliflower in Catania, very large heads in Naples. He lists a kind hardly ever found in our seed catalogs, *B. oleracea botrytis cymosa*, which has a thick, succulent stalk but negligible curds. The leaves and stalks of cauliflower are, of course, quite delicious, and are used in cauliflower soups by those who know.

Growing perfect cauliflower takes both thought and care. It does best in a moist, cool soil in climatic conditions where temperatures remain fairly even without wild plunges and leaps. A sheltering wall on the west side of the garden can do much to make a pleasant spot for cauliflower.

The very best seed should be used; don't buy drugstore seed packets, for the seed may be old and dried-out. If you save your own seed, choose only seed from plants with solid heads of regular shape to avoid offspring that grow into "buttons" or scraggly clumps. Choosing the right cultivar for your situation is a matter of trial and error. Sow three or four kinds each year and keep notes to find the ones that do best for you.

Because of the cauliflower's preference for cool temperatures as it begins to mature, growers try for both a very early crop and a late-season harvest. A better technique than starting the seeds indoors and transplanting to the garden is to start them outside under glass cloches, as the English do, in very early spring, so that a first crop is ready to harvest by late June. Fall crops are sown in June and July. Transplants are risky; if they are older than four or five weeks, they may not head up. Cauliflower also suffers transplant shock quite severely, and it takes the little plants up to two weeks to get back in shape; field-sown seedlings are usually ready to harvest a week or more before transplants set into the garden as much as fourteen days earlier are ready.

The fall crop can be a little tricky. The growing plants need even temperatures through the summer heat so that they will develop steadily. Shade cloths and mulch help. The fall crop is the main crop, and it will produce bigger heads than the early harvest. Professional growers make weekly sowings for a month in June or July to be sure of catching the right cool-down period in the fall for maximum quality. California growers can manage cauliflower in the winter. The Scandinavian countries grow very fine cauliflower under the midnight sun.

Cauliflower plants are thinned to stand about two feet apart. Steady, continuous growth is the secret of good heads, and that means regular supplies of adequate water. Rarely does cauliflower mature well by the grace of natural rainfall. A drought is disastrous and can force the heads into misshapen buttons.

Most cultivars are self-blanching, that is, they have large outer leaves that close around the head. Some cultivars, however, have looser, open leaves, and the gardener who is after a snow-white head may have to tie up these leaves—but *loosely*. A snug tie-up will cook the heads—a very common mistake that starting cauliflower growers make. Leave side openings and gaps for the sake of ventilation. It is also a good idea to open up tied leaves after a rain and let the head dry out. Trapped moisture can rot the cauliflower.

Cauliflowers, like the rest of the *Brassicae*, suffer from the attentions of cabbage loopers (*Trichoplusia ni*), the imported cabbage worm (*Pieris rapae*), and the caterpillar of the diamondback moth (*Plutella xylostella*). These scourges can be controlled with *Bacillus thuringiensis*, a species of bacterium that, when sprinkled on the affected plant, is eaten by the insect pest, which is then gradually paralyzed and dies. "B.t.", as it is called, is harmless to humans and is sold in most garden supply stores under several trade names, such as Dipel and Thuricide.

Cauliflower for crudités should be gathered a few hours before it will be served. The florets are cut from the head, blanched a few minutes in or over boiling water, then plunged into ice water. When they are cold and firm, they are drained and chilled for an hour or so in the refrigerator. Cauliflower florets treated this way will be crisp and tender, mild and beautiful, lending themselves in color and form to every kind of vegetable arrangement.

Although every seed house offers a few cauliflower cultivars, Stokes Seeds is something of a specialty store for cauliflower, offering seventeen cultivars to gardeners. Theirs is both a professional and a sentimental attachment, for the owner's father was a cauliflower grower during the Depression when he acquired the seed company. Danova has a large pure white head and holds for a long time. Delira is a European cauliflower that does not hold long, but has unique self-wrapping leaves that protect and blanch the head. Chartreuse is an unusual bright-green cauliflower-broccoli cross with a good flavor (offered by Blum Seeds).

Gardeners puzzled by the immense number of species in the insect world and their unceasing attention to the vegetable plots of humans will find *Rodale's Color Handbook of Garden Insects* by Anna Carr indispensable. There are three hundred action photographs of the insects—friend and foe—at their business. It is the most useful nonscholarly insect book around and also contains many recipes for organic weapons against the tribes of biting, chewing, sucking, egg-laying creatures.

One can fill many pages listing cauliflower cultivars. A sturdy and adaptable one is All the Year Round. Snow Crown, White Empress, Snowball, and dozens of other white-headed cauliflowers are easy to find. Less usual are the purple cauliflowers that turn green when they are cooked. Violet Queen, offered by Vermont Bean Seed, is a deep, rich purple color.

Flowering kale

(B. oleracea, Acephala group)

Flowering kales are stunning and dramatic in crudités. These handsome plants are greatly admired in the Far East, where gardeners grow gorgeously variegated rosettes in blue and gray-green embellished by frilly leaves and a spidery tracery of veins in bright pink, ashes-of-roses, cream, and mauve. But it is difficult to find packets of seed that give uniform cultivars in this country; seed usually comes in mixed colors. Some seed sellers are beginning to respond to gardeners' demands for the same color flowering kale in one packet to make the best effect in the garden. Some of the Japanese cultivars do just that; the rose and blue-gray of Feather-Leaved Coral Queen, and the blue-gray and white-veined Feather-Leaved Coral Prince can be bought from several companies. Harris offers a rather gaudy Red-on-Green cultivar, as does Park Seeds. Park also has two or three frizzy hybrids—Frizzy Red and Frizzy White. Although these beautiful plants are deliciously edible, they are never listed in the vegetable section of seed catalogs, but always with the flowers.

Flowering kales are hardy and do best in cool weather. The main crop is generally sown outdoors in late spring or early summer so that it can come to maturity in early fall. They are grown like cabbages and can stand some frost. Indeed, their flavor is better after a few light frosts. Flowering kale can be shredded in salads and cooked using any recipe for kale. They are good stuffed like savoy cabbage.

KOHLRABI

(*B. oleracea*, *Gongylodes* group)

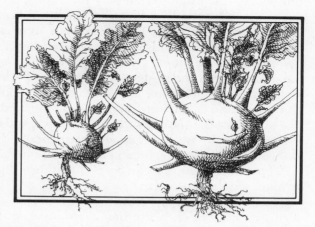

This curious vegetable looks like a turnip that has gone into a Dada stage, but it is actually one of the cabbage family. Its origins are obscure. Some scholars believe it was grown in prehistoric Europe, others that it was developed by the Romans, and yet others, including Sturtevant*, think it derives from the marrow cabbage. He says, "In 1884, two kohlrabi plants were growing in pots in the greenhouse at the New York State Agricultural Experiment Station; one of these extended itself until it became a marrow cabbage and when planted out in the spring attained its growth as a marrow cabbage." Readers who wish to know what a marrow cabbage is will be disappointed. Neither *Hortus* nor William Rhind nor Vilmorin tells us. Webster's Third Unabridged says only that it is *choumoellier*, a hybrid of the cabbage, kohlrabi, and kale! This explanation would give kohlrabi a truly unique ancestry that puts one in mind of a song popular in the 1940s called "I'm My Own Grandpa." Sturtevant, who obviously knew it well, gives us only tantalizing hints: it has a flat top and is very sensitive to cold.

At any rate, Sturtevant nails down Petrus Andrea Matthiolus as first noting, in his 1554 *Commentarii*, that the kohlrabi had but recently appeared in Italy. Gerard got seeds from Germany a little later, and kohlrabi grew in Edinburgh's Old Physic Garden before the end of the seventeenth century. M'Mahon listed it in 1806 in the United States, and by the time Vilmorin-Andrieux put together their great compendium of vegetables at the end of the nineteenth century, a number of kohlrabi cultivars were known—the White, the Purple, the Vienna, the Artichoke-Leaved, and the curly Neapoli-

---

*E. Lewis Sturtevant, first director of the New York Agricultural Experiment Station, and a tireless historian of edible plants. His notes, collected and edited by U.P. Hedrick as *Sturtevant's Notes on Edible Plants* (reprint edition, *Sturtevant's Edible Plants of the World* [New York: Dover Publications, 1972]), remains one of the great horticultural classics.

tan. Today it is usual to find only the white and purple types.

The plant is actually a biennial, though it is grown as an annual unless you are saving the seed. The fat, curious stem enlargement can be peeled and sliced raw for salads or cooked according to any celeriac recipe. The *Larousse Gastronomique* gives directions for *kohlrabi à la paysanne*, where the stem is sliced and sautéed with breast of pork and onion to which white wine and some stock are added. Kohlrabi is one of the better sources of vitamins A and C, calcium, phosphorus, iron, and several of the B vitamins. The quality of the stem is succulent, tender, and nutritious when the plant is young and the swellings about two inches in diameter. If the kohlrabi is allowed to grow larger, it can be pithy and tough. The crisp white flesh is very good eaten raw and can be cut into fancy shapes and served with a dip or plain with a little salt.

Like most cole crops, kohlrabi does best in cool weather, as a very early spring crop or an early autumn crop. Because the young plant can stand some frost, seed is usually sown directly in the bed, then thinned to stand six inches apart. Crowded kohlrabi will not develop the distinctive swollen stem. The plants can take partial shade and are even grateful for the coolness in the heat of summer. If you start young plants in midsummer for an autumn harvest, a shade cloth, regular watering, and heavy mulch will let them make steady growth without heat stress. Kohlrabi is a fast-growing plant and is ready for harvest twelve weeks after seed is sown. Successive seedings can give a long harvest period.

Almost every seed house offers kohlrabi; it's a puzzle why more people don't grow the handsome plant. Early White Vienna and Grand Duke are about the only cultivars found in our seed catalogs. They are similar in flavor, but the hybrid Grand Duke matures about ten days earlier than Vienna. A Purple Vienna is sometimes available from Harris Seeds.

BUNCHING ONIONS

**(*Allium fistulosum*, A. cepa x
A. fistulosum hybrids)**

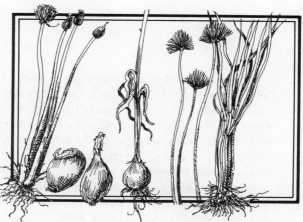

The *Allium* tribe is enormous, with four hundred odorous species in highly variable forms. The stout field onions come in many shapes and colors, in addition to clustered garlic cloves, slender chives, the airborne bulblets of Egyptian walking onions, the flat-leaved Chinese chives, thick-necked leeks, potato onions, and on and on and on. There are, says Parkinson, so many ways to use the various onions that "I cannot recount them, every one pleasing themselves, according to their order, manner or delight."

The marvelous onions are the most widely grown vegetable in the world, with a place in all cuisines. The mature, dry bulbs of *A. cepa* come in an extraordinary range of colors, vividly catalogued by Sturtevant as "white, dull white, silvery white, pearly white, yellowish green, coppery-yellow, salmon-yellow, greenish-yellow, bright yellow, pale salmon, salmon-pink, coppery-pink, chamois, red, bright red, blood-red, dark red, purplish."

The bunching onions are frequently misunderstood. They are quite different from the common bulb onions and are not just immature forms. The common onions have increasingly large underground bulbs and a few spindly leaves that give up and lie down late in summer. Bunching onions rarely bulb, and the massive clusters of fine blue-green leaves stand rich and sturdy well on into the autumnal frosts. Most of the group are ornamental as well as good in the kitchen. Some of the bunching onions are too strong to be enjoyed raw, and plants that are water-stressed will be very concentrated in flavor. Some of the pleasing and beautiful bunching onions that are handsome in the vegetable arrangement are rocambole, shallots, chives, Welsh onions, the flowering Chinese chives. In recent years seed catalogs have carried good selections of a whole new group of bunching onions from the orient; Ishikura Long Bunching, Kujo Green, Japanese Bunching are a few of these.

GLOBE ONIONS (*A. cepa*)

The globe onions, in their many colors, can be used in arrangements very effectively, and they are worth growing for their beauty alone. Strings of different-colored globe onions have long been braided and hung in kitchens from rafters and against the walls along with the bunches of dried herbs and *ristra*s of red or *mulato* chiles and garlic strings. All of these make a colorful autumn still life.

There are scores of remedies and old wives' tales associated with the onion family. Globe onions were used to foretell seasonal weather. One rhyme went:

Onion's skin very thin,
Mild winter coming in.
Onion skin thick and tough,
Coming winter cold and rough.

Snakes were supposed to dislike onions, and in snake-infested country, carrying a raw onion on one's person was supposed to ward them off.

There were a plethora of onion cures: chilblains rubbed with onion and salt (ouch!) were soon better; earache was eased with the help of a hot, roasted onion held against the ear; bald heads rubbed with onion and honey were supposed to sprout hair, and toothache could be cured by putting an onion skin on one's big toe.

Onions could decide which suitors were best. If a girl in old England was confused over which young man to marry, she scratched the initials of each swain on separate onions and then set the globes near the warm chimney. The first onion to sprout marked the best bridegroom.

Bunching onions are most often cut into brushes for crudités. In Japan even a mature globe onion is cut into many-petaled flowers for garnishes.

Bunching onions make perennial clumps that must be divided every few years. When they are first sown, the seed should be thickly strewn, for germination rates are often low. These plants enjoy rich, moist soil and full sun, but will generally tolerate conditions less than the ideal. They will often reseed themselves and are vigorous spreaders.

Rocambole (*A. sativum* var. *controversum*) is one of the most arresting of the group. This perennial is often erroneously listed as *A. scorodoprasum*. Its common name is serpent garlic, after its curious and handsome habit of making spiral twists in the stems that bear the flowers that later become aerial clusters of bulblets tinged faintly with purple. As the bulblets form, the stem straightens. The leaves are flat, like those of leeks. Rocambole is considered a native of the Caucasus Mountains and Syria. J. C. Loudon thought it native to Denmark, and the name rocambole is supposedly an anglicized version of the Danish *rockenbolle*, or "rock onion," for the plant grows there wild among the stony steeps. The little plant does not have much of a history and is only described from the sixteenth century on as a cultivated plant, but by 1726, Benjamin Townsend's gardening book, *The Complete Seedsman*, listed it as "mightily in request," and M'Mahon has it in his 1806 plant list.

The flavor of rocambole is closer to shallot than garlic, but it is distinctive in cookery to the connoisseur. Both the cloves of the underground swelling and the aerial bulblets can be used in the kitchen, although the underground bulbs are stronger in flavor. The twisting stems are used with great effect in vegetable groupings. The bulblets are usually planted in the fall for the next season's crop.

The only source of rocambole seeds that I know is Le Jardin du Gourmet.

CARROTS

(*Daucus carota*)

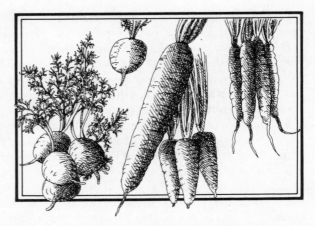

Carrots originated in southern Asia thousands of years ago. The wild carrot that grows today has thin, stringy roots, but has been described as aromatic and sweet. According to Sturtevant, wild carrots were still used in the late nineteenth century in the Hebrides and were "collected by the young women for distribution as dainties among their acquaintances on Sundays and at their dances."* William Rhind, in his *History of the Vegetable Kingdom*, remarks that the carrot was introduced into England by the Flemish during the reign of Queen Elizabeth I and was first grown near Sandwich, in Kent: "Parkinson, the celebrated botanist to James the first, mentions that in his time the ladies adorned their head-dresses with carrot-leaves, the light feathery verdure of which caused them to be no contemptible substitute for the plumage of birds."

The ancients apparently knew a domesticated form of the carrot, but often confounded it with the parsnip. Only in modern times has the vegetable become the plump, tasty root we know. In the late nineteenth century the famous French seed house Vilmorin-Andrieux of Paris conducted an experiment with the wild carrot to see what effects cultivation and selection would have. Says Sturtevant, "Vilmorin-Andrieux obtained in the space of three years roots as fleshy and large as those of the garden carrot from the thin, wiry roots of the wild species."

The shapes, sizes, and colors of carrots are quite variable, and may be the result of years of careful selection of regional types or may reflect differences in ancestral wild stock. The red carrots have a very deep ruddy orange coloring. (In the past, dairy farmers grew these not only because they made an excellent cattle feed but because the carotene gave the butterfat in the milk a deep, rich golden color. Health food addicts today who make a fetish of drinking large quantities of carrot juice have fallen subject to carotene-mia, or yellowing of the skin.) Carrot cultivars range from an almost trans-lucent white-fleshed carrot to innumerable shades of yellow and orange to red and purple.

For decades the market gardeners around Paris have made a good living by developing and growing very tender, sweet little carrots for the gourmet market. These are special cultivars that are diminutive when they are ma-ture, such as the Paris Market, French Horn, or Paris Forcing carrots—all pale, glossy vegetables nearly cylindrical in shape and only an inch or two long. The Nantes, an outstanding half-long type that developed in the neigh-borhood of Nantes in the last century, was an immediate garden favorite esteemed for its excellent flavor and remains the most important carrot to this day. Nantes strains and types dominate the carrot world.

Carrots from the Channel Islands, and from Belgium and Holland as well as France, have set the standards for table excellence. In the last few years several oriental cultivars have been attracting the attention of good cooks.

Growing carrots for a crudités display means keeping shapes and colors as well as good flavors in mind. All carrots are finer in flavor when pulled at early maturity. Big carrots that have lingered in the ground for weeks are better for cooking than for eating raw. But don't pull them too early either. The so-called baby carrots featured in gourmet food shops are not young and immature vegetables, but cultivars of small size when fully grown. Car-rots contain high levels of sugar and certain compunds called terpenoids, also found in pine needles and orange peel. Terpenoids are responsible for much of the carrot's flavor, but high levels of these pungent compounds give the root a soapy, sharp, disagreeable taste. Young carrots contain as much terpenoid as mature carrots, but it is more concentrated. Nor do young car-rots have good sugar levels. But when the carrot has grown for seven to nine weeks, it enters the mature stage and is at its peak flavor and full sugar level. Now is the time to pull them and enjoy them.

It is not only young carrots that can have disagreeable levels of terpen-oids. Some cultivars, bred for size or bright color or keeping qualities, may be very inferior in flavor, texture, or both.

It is possible to find more than fifty different carrot cultivars, most of them Nantes derivatives, just leafing through the seed catalogs. It is the cultivar, above all else, that determines mature carrot flavor. Specialty car-rot seed for the cook's garden might include Belgium White, a mild-fla-vored, pure-white carrot, generally used for casseroles in France and the Low Countries, but undeniably a novelty in the edible vegetable display. Touchon is a medium-size, bright-red-orange coreless French carrot, much esteemed for its flavor. Nugget is a solid-orange, almost round, little carrot. The cylindrical shape is eye-catching, and the short root makes this cultivar suitable for clay soils that would deform longer types. Nugget and other round carrots can be grown in pots and containers. The Baby Long is another carrot with an interesting shape and good flavor. It is a very slender carrot that is mature when it is six or seven inches long but only half to three-quarters of an inch in diameter. Carrot Sucram is a small Nantes-type carrot with high sugar levels. These are the so-called baby carrots in jars at terrible prices in the fancy imported-food aisles. Seeds of these cultivars can be ordered from Nichols Garden Nursery.

The Urban Farmer carries ten carrot cultivars, including the little round Paris Market and Touchon. Little Fingers is another "baby"-carrot type with high sugar content; it is only three or four inches long when mature. Vriends Glorie from Holland is a bright-orange, very sweet, medium-size carrot with outstanding flavor. Urban Farmer also offers two carrot samplers, each with generous samples of five different cultivars.

J.A. Demonchaux carries the outstanding European "gourmet" carrot Amstel, a sweet little cultivar half an inch through and three or four inches long at six weeks, when it should be pulled and eaten raw.

Thompson and Morgan carries an excellent selection of carrots with a pictograph profile chart. Of interest to the crudités grower is Juwarot, a good-flavored carrot with exceptionally high levels of vitamin A.* The tiny Suko is mature when only two and a half inches long and is considerably smaller than an average-size string bean. It is sweet and tender and when bunched and tied in thick clusters, then turned upside down, it looks like a spider crysanthemum.

Among Japanese carrots worth trying are Senko, an extremely slim, deep-orange carrot that can reach twenty inches in length in a well-prepared bed. *Well-prepared* means double-dug to two feet, of enriched, mellow, loamy soil. This spectacular carrot may take a little fussing in order to get smooth; tapering, straight roots, but the game is worth the candle. J. L. Hudson carries Senko, and Redwood City has the similar Kokubu.

Every year there are new hybrid carrots out, mostly of the Nantes type, mostly medium-size, uniform vegetables with heavy yields and fairly good flavor. Carrot fanciers usually spurn hybrids but reports have it that Clarion is an early, very sweet, delicious carrot. It is carried by Johnny's Selected Seeds.

---

*Juwarot has the *highest* Vitamin A content ever recorded in carrots, according to the note in *The Garden Seed Inventory* (ed. Kent Whealy [Decorah, Iowa: Seed Saver Publications, 1985], p. 132).

Red Muscade is a European carrot much grown in North Africa. It is a medium-size root that stays sweet in hot weather when other cultivars turn bitter and sharp. It is a good carrot for southern gardeners and can be sown in late summer for a fall and winter harvest. Le Marché has it.

The people who save vegetable seeds and collect unusual cultivars are among the most interesting gardeners around. Collecting old cultivars and new types leads one inevitably into taste comparisons. Collectors usually have sophisticated palates. Members of Kent Whealy's Seed Savers Exchange know, grow, and eat some of the most delicious vegetable cultivars in the world, many of them unknown outside a small circle and unavailable from commercial sources. Quite a few gardeners collect carrot cultivars. Some specialize in carrot colors other than orange, some in endangered carrot varieties, others in giant carrots only.

James Whitman of Tacoma, Washington, is a psychologist who grows and collects carrots. He has more than thirty cultivars. Some are commercially available and have certain desirable characteristics. Whitman names Demi-Long Nantes from Spain as having "exceptional flavor"; grows Juwarot, which he selected for flavor; and remarks that Sucram is "gourmet quality," as is Amstel.

An enormous carrot that is distinguished for its size rather than its flavor is Zino, available from Thompson and Morgan. This huge root is listed in the *Guinness Book of Records* as having produced the largest carrot in the world, a record-breaking seven-pound eleven-and-a-half ounce monster.

Growing Extraordinary Carrots

Carrots are a half-hardy crop that can stand some mild spring frost, and may be sown two to four weeks before the last spring freezes. Fifty feet of garden row will yield approximately forty-five pounds of carrots. Generally two crops of carrots are planted—the first sowing in mid-spring, and a second sowing in mid-summer for a fall crop.

Carrot seed germinates slowly, and can take several weeks to emerge. Presprouting and fluid gel sowing are useful. Many gardeners plant radish seed with the carrot seed. The radishes emerge first, loosening the soil and helping the carrot seedlings emerge more easily. The carrot bed should be watered daily until the little plants come up. Drought will delay germination.

Carrots like a mellow, loamy soil without stones. The pH should be around 6.5, and lime should be added, if necessary, weeks before planting to bring the pH up to a good level. Clay soils or compacted soils are poor mediums for raising fine carrots. Not only do the seedlings have great difficulty forcing their way out of this soil as it crusts over, but the roots cannot grow straight, and tend to fork. Fresh manure should not be put on a carrot bed, for it stimulates root forking and causes rough skin and flabby flesh.

Carrot seed should be sown fairly thickly, five or six seeds per inch, then thinned out later unless you sow radish seed at the same time. A thick scattering of carrot seed helps make emergence rates better, because the combined thrust of many seedlings against the soil crust breaks it open. Thin carrot seedlings to stand one every two or three inches.

Carrot crops should be part of a good rotation system to avoid the carrot rust fly or soft rot. Rust fly larvae overwinter in the soil and hit the second year's crop if you plant it in the same place. Carrot yellows is a disease transmitted by the six-spotted leafhopper, and the disease absolutely ruins the flavor of the roots, making them bitter and astringent.

Carrots can be mulched heavily in the fall with straw, leaves, or soil and dug out during the winter as wanted. They may also be stored in damp sand in a root cellar. The flavor of carrots stored this way is not prime, but they are still edible. Carrot fanciers will prefer to grow pots or larger containers of the small carrots inside on the windowsill during the winter. Even an apartment gardener can enjoy the delectable, crisp-fleshed quality carrot in the dead of winter, and these are truly treasures to arrange on a silver dish.

CELERIAC

(Apium graveolens var. rapaceum)

Celeriac is one of the chic new vegetables that have appeared on the gourmet produce counters in the last few years. There is an amazing difference between the flabby, stale celeriac that has languished for weeks in a bin while suspicious shoppers wonder what it is and the fresh, firm roots we dig from the garden to use in salads, in *céleri-râve à la paysanne* or crisp-fried julienne with parsley.

Celeriac is a biennial species of celery with a large, white root. The leaves and small, hollow stems are powerfully strong in taste and used only in soups and sauces. The fleshy, turniplike tuber ends with a tangle of tiny rootlets like Medusa's hairdo.

There were once many celeriac cultivars grown in France and Germany, from the large, ten-ounce *céleri-râve ordinaire* to the tiny Tom Thumb Erfurt with a tuber no bigger than a walnut. The *ordinaire* was a lumpy, large, rather grotesque vegetable, but the Erfurt type was smooth, shaped like a tiny apple, and with fewer rootlets underneath. Sturtevant notes that Giambattista Porta, a Neapolitan polymath of the sixteenth century, describes a celeriac, in his 1592 *Villae*, of a size unknown today. Sturtevant translates the passage thus:

> There is another kind of celery called Capitatum, which is grown in the gardens of St. Agatha, Theano and other places in Apulia, granted from nature and unseen and unnamed by the ancients. Its bulb is spherical, nearly of the size of a man's head. It is very sweet, odorous and grateful. Except in rich land, it degenerates, until it differs from the common apium in no respects, except its root, round like a head.

What a pity that one disappeared!

In France, celeriac is most often cooked in butter or puréed, and sometimes stuffed for an unusual and handsome garnish. In Germany, it is cooked as any other root vegetable, added to soups, sliced, or grated into salads. The flavor is celerylike, but richer and milder, a kind of buttery, nutlike celery taste.

Generally the only kinds of celeriac available through our seed catalogs are Prague, a large, rough root that is hard to peel, and the newer Alabaster from Holland, a little bigger than Prague and less lumpy in shape. Both are available from many seed houses without too much searching. In addition, Urban Farmer carries another Holland cultivar called Zwijndrechtse Zwinda. Epicure has De Reuil, which has a finer texture than Prague. Nichols is the only seed house at present that carries Dolvi, a new disease-resistant celeriac of considerable size and smooth, round shape. Harris has Marble Ball, a thick-knobbed celeriac with very few side roots.

Growing Extraordinary Celeriac

The seed catalogs tell us that celeriac is easier to grow than celery. That's true, if you happen to have just the right climatic conditions. Celeriac has the same general needs as celery, but it *must* have cool growing-season temperatures with a monthly mean temperature range of between 60 and 65 degrees F. Where temperature averages are higher than 70 to 75 degrees F the crop will fail or be just marginal.

Like celery and parsley, celeriac seed is slow to germinate, and germination rates are generally low. Presoaking the seed helps. Sow the seeds heavily and start them inside eight to ten weeks before the frosts end in your garden. It is very important not to set celeriac outdoors too soon, for nighttime temperatures that drop below 45 degrees F can trigger the plant's biennial urge to send up seed stalks instead of putting the energy into a plump delicious root. The young plants should, of course, be hardened off before they are set out.

Celeriac seedlings are placed four to six inches apart in rows two or more feet apart. If they are set in beds, allow at least a foot between plants.

"...NOT WORTHY OF MUCH ATTENTION..."

One suspects Joseph Harris, the founder of Harris Seeds, may have set his celeriac out too soon, for he wrote gloomily in the 1879 catalog, "I either do not know how to raise celeriac or turnip rooted celery, or it is not worthy of much attention; it is useful, perhaps, for flavoring soups, etc."

Loamy, sandy soils with a shot of potassium are favored by celeriac, and it, like celery, needs plenty of water. If it is not watered regularly and mulched, the plants can become tough and woody. A shot of manure tea every ten days or so makes big, firm roots.

Gardeners who have grown celeriac for years suggest cutting off the rootlets that grow outward near the top of each tuber to keep it from being misshapen. The protruding tops of the tubers should be covered over with earth during the last few weeks before harvest.

You can start digging up the tubers when they are two and a half inches in diameter. Celeriac will grow up to four inches across, but the larger it is, the coarser and more woody the flesh. The finest flavors and textures belong to the smaller, more youthful celeriacs.

To use raw celeriac in the crudités, peel it and cut it into engaging shapes. The round slices lend themselves to fan and palm branch forms.

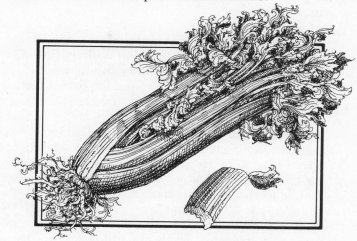

CELERY

(Apium graveolens var. dulce)

The *Apium* group is made up of about twenty subspecies of herbs native to North and South America, Australia, Eurasia, and New Zealand. Celery probably originated in low-lying, swampy areas near the eastern Mediterranean. The *selinon* of the Odyssey is thought to be a wild celery, or "smallage," a strong-flavored, aromatic plant. The ancients seem to have grown the pungent plant in their "physic gardens" for medicinal use rather than as a food, and it is not until the seventeenth century that smallage got into the kitchen garden as a flavorful addition to soups and broths. At the turn of the century a smallage very similar to the wild plant was still grown in France, called *céleri à couper*, or cutting celery. This small plant had hollow stems.

The first reference to the word *celery* is in a ninth-century poem, *Hortulus*, by Walafrid Strabo. In it, Strabo listed the medicinal virtues of *Apium* and wrote "*Passio tum celeri cedit devicta medelae*," which Sturtevant translates as meaning "the disease then to celery yields, conquered by the remedy," but adds that the word *celeri* here carries the meaning as well of "quick acting," from the Latin *celeriter*.

A domesticated celery seems to have been grown first in Tuscany, and in 1686 John Ray wrote in his *Historia plantarum*, "smallage transferred to culture becomes milder and less ungrateful, when in Italy and France the leaves and stalks are esteemed as delicacies, eaten with oil and pepper."

Green celery was always favored in Italy, but in later centuries in England and North America, the plants were blanched to produce mild white stalks. There were at one time hollow-stalked celeries, and English agriculture writer William Cobbett thought this the best kind of all. Today it has disappeared.

Celeries can be green, red, golden, or pink, but the more unusual colors are rarely available commercially. One red celery of the past grew to an enormous size and is described in William Rhind's *History of the Vegetable Kingdom*: "A head of celery was dug up in 1815, in the neighborhood of Manchester, which weighed nine lbs. when washed, with the roots and leaves all attached to it, and measured ten feet six inches in height. It was of a red sort, perfectly solid, crisp, firm, and remarkably well-flavored." Vilmorin-Andrieux lists a Manchester Red among its celery cultivars in 1885, and we may guess the strain came from that vigorous giant. Most of the celeries listed in *The Vegetable Garden* a hundred years ago were white-stalked types that had to be blanched. Dwarf white cultivars were popular both in Europe and this country, and Harris's 1879 seed catalog lists three white celeries, including Turner's Incomparable Dwarf White. Wrote the original Joseph Harris in the catalog text, "For my own use I grow this variety exclusively; I know of nothing better."

The sad news is that there is a very limited choice of celery cultivars today. Three types dominate the seed catalogs. Giant Pascal is a long-season Utah strain, a rich-green, vigorous plant that takes more than 120 days to reach maturity. Utah 52-70R is another popular dark-green celery, both vigorous and dependable. Both Giant Pascal and Utah are widely grown commercially. Golden Self-Blanching is the third member of this dominant trio. This is a yellow-stalked celery and is much favored in England, where the tradition of white blanched celery lives on. Golden Self-Blanching is a clear yellow color close to the glowing gold of wax beans. It has a fine, mild, nutty flavor, less pronounced than the green types. Bountiful Gardens has Solid White, a handsome exhibition celery of pale color.

Harris offers Summer Pascal, an improved green cultivar developed at the University of Massachusetts for eastern soils. It is a brittle, thick-stemmed celery that resists bolting and has a very good flavor. It is juicy and crisp. The plants tend to flare out as they develop. Johnny's Selected Seeds sells a commercial hybrid celery called Green Giant that has some resistance to blight and mosaic (diseases not likely to be encountered in the home garden). The flavor is not particularly exciting, though the stalks are thick and juicy.

Several seedsmen sell red celery. Thompson and Morgan has Red Giant, a purple-tinged hardy celery that takes on a pink flush when earthed up to blanch it. J. L. Hudson has a similar kind, Solid Red. Celery listings in the Seed Savers yearbook for the winter of 1984 include Brydon's Prize Pink and Brydon's Prize Red, as well as several regional wild celeries.

The French *céleri à couper*, or cutting celery, is sold through Nichols, William Dam, Thompson and Morgan, and others for flavoring soups, stews, and casseroles. This strong-flavored dwarf plant is often listed as French Celery Dinant.

In selecting a suitable strain you might be interested to know that green varieties have more vitamins than blanched types.

Growing Extraordinary Celery

Celery has the reputation of being a hard crop to grow. Part of this reputation lingers from the days when elaborate blanching procedures were needed to make the mild, ivory-white stalks then in vogue. Those older varieties had to have a rich, damp soil. The shift to green types of self-blanching cultivars, as well as the breeders' work to bring out cultivars more tolerant of different types of soil, makes growing celery within the compass of many home gardeners.

Celery seed should be started indoors in soil cubes eight to twelve weeks before the plants are to be set out in the garden. All danger of frost must be past at this time, and the young celery plants should be six inches high. The garden soil in the celery bed is prepared several weeks before the young plants are set out.

Celery needs a long, cool growing season in fertile, damp soil. Commercial growers plant it in enriched muck soil. The ideal growing temperature for celery is in the 60- to 70-degree range; if the temperature goes above this point even for a short period, the stalks get tough and very strongly flavored. This is why so much home-grown celery is intensely flavored, especially by midsummer when it may create an almost burning sensation in the mouth. Many home gardeners have been put off trying to grow it a second time. Some of the difficulty in keeping celery plants cool and moist is eased by growing them in partial shade, whether natural tree shade that falls over the celery plot in the hottest part of the day or from a good shade cloth. Drip irrigation keeps them damp and happy.

The older types of celery have long seasons of 120 days, but newer celery types mature in eighty-five days. In the North, celery is grown as a summer and fall harvest crop, but in the South, gardeners plant it for winter and spring harvest.

Celery-bed soil is conditioned with compost and enriched with nitrogen, potash, phosphate, or with rotted stable, sheep, or chicken manure. A pH range of 6.0 to 7.5 is ideal for celery. The enriched soil should be dug and mixed until a bed at least fourteen inches deep is ready, then heavily watered and allowed to stand a week or ten days before the young plants are set in. Celery growth should be rapid and steady, and that means a constant, even supply of water and food.

The young plants are spaced six inches apart in the row, or twelve inches apart in the bed. Have the watering can by your elbow as you set them out and use it liberally. After the plants are all in, water them again. Mulch the plants heavily to hold in the moisture. (Very few vegetable transplants should be mulched right after they are set out. Celery is an exception.) Water the plants heavily every few days to get them going and continue to water three or four times a week throughout their entire growing period to give them firm crisp texture and mild flavor. Manure tea should be given the plants once a week.

If you are growing one of the older varieties, it is not difficult to blanch them. When the plants are about eighteen inches tall, wrap them in heavy white butchers' waxed paper, allowing six inches of green leaves to emerge from the top. Do *not* use newspaper or brown paper, for both give the celery off-flavors. Heap earth up around the bottom of the paper cone to hold it firmly in place. Blanch the plants for ten days to four weeks, depending on your fancy, and continue to water and feed them as they mature.

In the nineteenth century, gardeners dug deep trenches and set the young plants out in them. Gradually the trenches were filled in with soil. This procedure kept the plants in sufficient moisture and blanched them as they grew. It was cool in the trench, too. It is a lot of work, but is still one way to grow large, tender, pale, celery. A drawback is that soil gets into the hearts of the plants.

If frosts threaten to come on before your celery is ready, mulch the plants heavily with straw or dry bracken fern and hope for Indian summer.

Harvesting celery for immediate use means cutting the plant off just below the surface of the ground. If you wish to store it into the winter in the root cellar (and celery stores very well), dig up the plants up with the root system largely intact, then pack them in straw in boxes before bringing them into the cool cellar.

CUCUMBERS
(*Cucumis sativus*)

A tender annual vine with origins in southern Asia, the familiar cucumber supports itself with clinging tendrils. Cucumbers are cultivated plants of antiquity and have been recognizably identified in a fifth-century Chinese agricultural treatise. The Romans grew them as great delicacies, and the emperor Tiberius enjoyed forced fruits of the cucumber vine all through the year. Cucumbers were included in the list of select vegetables and fruits that Charlemagne ordered grown on his estates. In ancient Egypt and Syria, writes the indefatigable William Rhind, there was the curious occupation known as cucumber watcher, a man who spent his time in "large open fields, in which a hut was erected for the abode of the watchman, who guarded the fruit against foxes and jackals."*

Although cucumbers were common in medieval England, their culture and harvest were neglected during the tedious War of the Roses, and the plants were reputedly lost from English gardens for more than one hundred years. But the 1633 edition of Gerard's great *Herball* says, "there be divers sorts of Cucumbers; some greater, some lesser: some of the garden, some wilde; some of one fashion, and some of another." These fruits are cold in nature and were used by our ancestors not only in salads but as exterior poultices in conjunction with other ingredients for "parts troubled with heat." Gerard lists a few of these afflictions as "red and shining fierie noses (as red as red Roses) with pimples, pumples, rubies and such like."

Antoine Le Grand wrote on natural history in the seventeenth century, and he claimed that very tender and delicate cucumbers could be grown if the seed were soaked in milk before it was sown. And no less a personage than Francis Bacon, in a discussion of potions and procedures that prolong life, lists cucumbers sliced in milk as one of many ingredients in "Methusalem water."

Nicholas Culpeper made a nice point on the pronunciation of cucumber; only the vulgar, he says, say, "cowcumber." John Evelyn, that ardent champion of the salad bowl, was a devotee of the cucumber, whether mixed into the larger salad composition or dressed alone with any of several piquant sauces. In winter, he wrote in his *Acetaria*, they could be enjoyed as pickles.

Christopher Columbus planted cucumbers in Haiti on the 1494 voyage, but early explorers and settlers in the New World noted many times that cucumbers were widely grown by the Indians. Jacques Cartier at the site of Montreal, Hernando de Soto in Florida, Captain John Smith in Virginia— all named cucumbers as one of the vegetables of native Indian culture.

Not everyone loves cucumbers. A disgruntled gentleman, described by William Rhind only as "the late Mr. Abernethy," was such an individual. He had "a quaint receipt for their use, which was to peel off the cucumber, slice it, pepper it, put vinegar to it, and then throw it out at the window."

Cucumbers, despite the Mr. Abernethys of the world, became indispensable to modern life; they were grown in great fields in Europe, in hotbeds, in market gardens to satisfy the yearnings of consumers. The cucumber has always enjoyed considerable variation in form, but in the nineteenth century, Vilmorin-Andrieux listed the little brown-skinned netted Russian cucumber; the Bonneuil White, grown in Paris environs for use in perfumes; the Dutch Yellow; Rollisson's Telegraph, which produced fruits sixteen inches long; and the Duke of Edinburgh, whose stupendous cucumber namesakes attained thirty inches in length. The Green Chinese and the knobbly little pickling gherkins were on the list, along with curious cucumbers such as the Snake (*Cucumis melo*), a slender, curled, and twisted cucurbit, highly variable in shape and often with a musky scent, and *C. anguria*, or the West Indian gherkin, also called the Bur Gherkin or Gooseberry Gourd for its prickly fruits, which were savored as pickles.

A great deal of breeding work has been done with cucumbers in the last fifty years. There are now available to the gardener cucumbers with multiple disease resistance. The new gynodioecious cucumber plants have only female flowers, and the result is heavy yields and a concentrated period of fruiting. These characteristics are boons for the commercial producer but do not necessarily mean better-flavored fruits. Monoecious cucumbers, which bear both male and female flowers, will fruit throughout a longer season and are better for the salad gardener, who rarely wants his whole crop at once. Another new cucumber direction has been the development of parthenocarpic cucumbers, which are seedless. These odd things produce fruit without being pollinated or setting seed. They are quite long in shape and have only appeared in the markets in the last few years at astronomical prices, largely because until quite recently they were grown in greenhouses abroad. Growers here are now planting cultivars that combine gynodioecious and parthenocarpic traits and allow the seedless cucumber to be field-grown as long as standard cucumbers are remote enough in distance to discourage cross-pollinating visits by busy bees.

Cucumbers are generally classed as either slicers or picklers. Slicers are medium to large in size, whereas picklers tend to be short and stout. Both are good for crudités when young and fine-fleshed. Sweet Slice is a slender, burpless cucumber of superior flavor. It does not have to be peeled and grows up to twelve inches long. Vermont Bean Seed and many others have it. Sweet Success is one of the new gynodioecious-parthenocarpic hybrids, a sweet, crisp, seedless cucumber of excellent flavor, carried by Nichols Garden Nursery. It was a 1983 All-American Selections winner, an indication that it grows well in all parts of the country. The Yard Long Armenian Cucumber is a thin, very long vegetable of good quality, much grown in California. Both J. L. Hudson and Nichols Garden Nursery have it. Apple Crystal (sometimes listed as the Lemon Cucumber) is white and round and mild; J. L. Hudson, Johnny's Selected Seeds, and others carry it under either of its common names.

Oriental cucumbers are seen here and there on the market. A striking and slender cucumber for imaginative arrangements is the Kyoto, a very spiny, somewhat grotesquely curled fruit up to twenty-four inches long. Urban Farmer has this and three other oriental cucumbers.

There has been a good deal of gardener interest in pickling cucumbers suitable for making *cornichons*, the little sour pickles served with pâté. Both Nichols Garden Nursery and Le Marché carry Cucumber Cornichon de Bourbonne, and both include a recipe for pickling the tiny cukes. Nichols also has seed of the hard-to-find West India Gherkin, the bur-cucumber mentioned above.

Cucumbers are frost-tender and should not be planted until all frosts are past. Seed may be started inside in soil blocks four weeks before the end of the frost period. It is important that the seedling roots not be pulled or disturbed in transferring from the starting flat to the garden. Cucumbers cannot tolerate weeds, and they need considerable water to keep them growing steadily, the secret of perfect fruits. Water stress causes them to drop blossoms, make poor fruit-set, and produce deformed and bitter cucumbers.

Cucumbers will produce fruits six to eight weeks after they are planted.

To keep them coming, they should be kept picked. Letting them swell into gross yellow monsters will signal the plant that its job is done and it's time to quit.

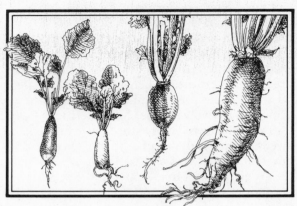

RADISH

(Raphanus sativus spp.)

Older authorities believed the radish originated in China, but it was extensively grown in ancient Egypt, Greece, and Rome. The Greeks thought the radish so fine that in offerings to Apollo radishes made of gold were laid before the god, while beets rated only silver, and turnips, lead. By the sixteenth century, Gerard could name a number of radish cultivars: black, white, long, round, and pear-shaped. They were eaten raw "with bread in stead of other food...But for the most part they are used as a sauce with meates to procure appetite." John Parkinson, in his 1629 *Paradisi in Sole, Paradisus Terrestris* of the punning title, said radishes "do usually serve as a *stimulum* before meat, and ... the poor eat them alone with bread and salt." John Evelyn, wit, savant, and ardent horticultural writer of the seventeenth century, remarked in his rich treatise on salads, *Acetaria*, that the best radishes were "the young Seedling Leaves and Roots, raised on the Monthly Hotbed almost the whole Year round."

One of the most famous seed lists is a bill dated 26 July 1631, made out by Robert Hill, a London grocer, to John Winthrop, Jr., the son of colonial governor John Winthrop. The seeds of sixty plants, vegetables, herbs, and flowers, were on this list and included "8 oz Radish seed at 12d per li." By 1806, Bernard M'Mahon could list ten radish cultivars grown here in his *The American Gardener's Calendar*.

Radishes are generally divided into three basic groups: the tender table delicacies known as forcing or spring radishes; the slower-growing, heavier, summer and autumn types; and the oriental winter and spring radishes called daikon, characterized by their deep, hard, and very large roots.

The spring radish types, particularly useful in crudités, are diverse in color and form. They may be round, turnip-shaped, long and tapering, olive-shaped, or pear-shaped. The colors are yellow, scarlet, white, salmon, lilac, purple, pink, and even two- or three-toned. Late-season radishes tend to be more pungent than the juicy, mild spring types and are generally the long tapering shapes of parsnips, or the round, flat-bottomed turnip shapes. They can be yellow, gray, white, red, black, or purple. Aside from the oriental winter radishes, there are a number of these large, late-season types, such as Black Spanish, Chinese Scarlet, and Russian White.

Vilmorin-Andrieux, in addition to more than fifty radish cultivars in all these groups (except daikon), included some specialties. Noteworthy were Mans Corkscrew, a twisty root, and de Mahon, "an exceedingly distinct kind, peculiar to the Balearic Islands and some districts in the south of France. It is a Long Red Radish, the root being often angular . . . and projecting from the ground for one-half or two-thirds of its length. . . . The flesh is pinkish white, very juicy, firm, and solid while young." Rond Rouge Foncé is another particular variety "which has a very dark, almost violet-colored skin. It is rather in repute in the southern provinces of France." The Triumph was a beautiful flattened white globe streaked horizontally and shot through with scarlet bands, and Early Yellow was a bright ocher. The big market radish in Paris was the French Breakfast Radish, still highly esteemed by radish fanciers. Vilmorin-Andrieux said of it:

Under this name two distinct varieties are grown, differing from each other not only in colour, but also in productiveness, etc. The *Parisian strain* is a very handsome variety, . . . skin a florid and rather lively pink on the upper part—four-fifths—of the root, and white on the lower part. Like the White-tipped Scarlet Turnip Radish, this variety is exceedingly early; but the root very soon becomes hollow if it is not pulled as soon as it is fully formed. It grows much better in a hot-bed, or in compost or leaf-mould, than in ordinary garden soil.

The kind known as the *Southern strain* is rather thicker and longer in the root than the Parisian, and the pink colour is not quite so bright, and one-fourth of the root is white. The greater size of the white blotch of this variety distinguishes it sufficiently, and it has the advantage of being well suited for sowings during the summer in the open ground.*

The radish is still a popular and well-appreciated hors d'oeuvre in France, served fresh and young on a plate with a few of the more shapely leaves attached, to accompany crusty French bread and sweet butter. In this country gardeners most often grow the Cherry Belle, a nice enough spring radish from Holland, but only the tip of the radish iceberg. Wonderful and unusual radish types can be unearthed in the catalogs, and these add great interest and color to crudités.

Le Marché has the European Sezanne, a pale-pink-and-white globe radish, tender and juicy, and ready to eat three weeks after the seed is sown. Bountiful Gardens has French Breakfast, and the late-season bright-pink China Rose, a longer, stronger-flavored radish that takes several months to mature. The Urban Farmer offers a German spring radish, Delikat (a long red with a white tip), and two winter radishes from Germany, where they are greatly liked. These are Langer Schwarzer Winter (Long Black Winter radish) and the famous accompaniment to black bread and dark beer, the Münchener Bier radish. Epicure has several German radishes, and a spring type from Holland, Saxafire. Johnny's Selected Seeds carries Easter Egg, a novelty spring radish of four colors—red, pink, purple, and white—as well as several crimson types and the good old White Icicle, with its fine, almost translucent flesh. These Icicles should always be harvested when they are young.

Nichols Garden Nursery has French Breakfast and four other spring radishes. Hailstone is a large white globe radish with an excellent, delicate, even sweet, flavor. A real prize is the French Golden radish, which has a deep, glowing gold color and unique and very good flavor. Le Jardin du Gourmet and Thompson and Morgan both have Pontvil Oblong, a strain of the French Breakfast radish that holds longer and stays firm instead of going hollow. An unusually beautiful radish is Violet de Gournay, a deep-purple-skinned winter radish available both from Seed Saver Glenn Drowns, and from Nichols Garden Nursery.

Growing Extraordinary Radishes

It is not easy to grow a truly fine radish—succulent, tender, crackling crisp and mild in flavor—though children and beginning gardeners are always told to throw some of the "foolproof" seeds into the ground and then

---

*Incidentally, Vilmorin and Andrieux were two men, partners in the Paris seed company, but I've never been able to find their first names. They seem linked together in history and book as Vilmorin-Andrieux.

wait for the crop. The result is usually a stringy, palate-stinging root not worth pulling. The French perfected the art of growing spring radishes for the Paris market. They forced them very early in the season in glass-covered beds of fine, rich loam or compost.

Radishes *must* have cool weather and fertile, moist, cool soil if they are to be good. If they are stressed for water or grown in hot weather, they become tough, stringy, and pungently "hot." Long summer days and warm weather make them bolt rapidly to seed. They should be grown in earliest spring, or in fall, or in the shade.

Some gardeners prepare beds in the fall and sow radishes in the cold frame as soon as the snow is gone; others wait a week or ten days and sow in the open ground as soon as the soil can be worked. Southern gardeners sow in the early- and late-winter months.

Sow radish seed thinly, one seed every two or three inches. Thick clumps of seedlings inhibit root development and deform some of the roots at a very tender age. The seed is sown one-quarter to one-half inch deep, but no deeper. The soil covering over the seed should be firmly pressed in place, for the earth pressure encourages the seedlings to make a plump bulb more quickly.

Radishes take only a few weeks to grow and should be grown as quickly and evenly as possible to reach perfection. The lingering radish that develops slowly is usually not good. Frequent watering is important for quick growth. Weeding is vital, for the radishes will lose quality if threatened by other plants for room and water.

Radishes are frequently intercropped with other species, but if they are sown with slow-germinating carrot or parsley, they should not be forgotten there, but pulled from the bed before they shade out the slower plants. A favorite place for radishes is in the asparagus bed, where they go very well in the rich, deep loam.

As spring radishes are pulled, more are planted every ten days or so until the weather gets too warm. Summer crops of passably good radishes are possible if seed is sown in a cool, partially shaded piece of ground.

Late-summer or autumn radishes have the same needs as spring types, but they take longer to develop and can stand some heat. They should not be stressed for water. A shade cloth or mulch will help hold moisture in and cool the soil.

The winter radishes are sown in May or June for a late-fall or early-winter harvest. These are more pungent than other types and must have good water throughout the growing season or they will be too hot and coarse for pleasure, even with black bread and strong beer. Mulch helps.

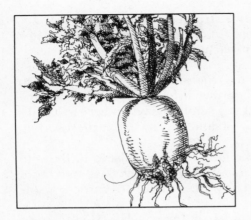

Daikon, the Japanese Radish (*R. sativus* var. *longipinnatus*)

The most popular of all vegetables in Japan is the giant radish, or *daikon*, the Japanese word that includes all these big fellows. Daikon, like the tiny relative grown here and in Europe, comes in spring-maturing strains that are mild and grow rapidly, as well as in winter- or fall-harvest cultivars that may be very pungent and take several months to mature. Daikon has many culinary uses that are attractive to Western gardener-cooks. It is often cut or grated into fine threads as a *digestif* accompanying other dishes. It is cut into paper-thin slices that show a graceful starry pattern. The slices can be served with a number of pungent or spicy sauces. Daikon is also cut in fanciful shapes by Japanese chefs skilled in the garnishing arts. The great roots are fermented in rice bran in Japan to make a fine "pickle" of unique taste that is somewhat chewy, somewhat crisp, and of a deep-yellow color.

A great interest in these big roots has inflamed North American gardeners if we judge by the dozen or more cultivars now available through our seed houses. The Kitazawa Seed Company in San Jose, California, specializes in oriental vegetables and offers no less than nine kinds of daikon. Of particular interest are Shogoin, a white winter globe up to seven inches in diameter, crisp, tender, and somewhat pungent, but very good with cream dips. Don't be tempted by Sakurajima, an even larger globe that can weigh up to fifty pounds when grown by fanatics who strive for enormity. (The same cult of the gigantic afflicts pumpkin growers, who ignore all qualities except that of great size.) Sakurajima is too pungent to be enjoyed raw. Minowase is an early-summer daikon, ready in about fifty days, that grows eighteen inches long and is mildly pungent in flavor and somewhat heat and disease resistant.

Redwood City has four spring daikons, including Minowase, and six winter types, among them Shogoin, hot Sakurajima, and the big Awa pickling daikon. William Dam has Nerima, the longest of all daikons, whose roots can extend thirty inches down. Chinese White Celestial and Takinashi are mild and good.

HELP WITH COOKING ORIENTAL VEGETABLES

Good and authentic recipes, such as Radish Pudding, Winter Soup, Braised Beef and Radish, are found in Martha Dahlen and Karen Phillipps's *A Popular Guide to Chinese Vegetables* (New York: Crown Publishers, 1983). This well-illustrated paperback combines two earlier books, *A Guide to Chinese Market Vegetables*, and its sequel, *A Further Guide to Chinese Market Vegetables*. Both made a great hit with Westerners living in Hong Kong before *A Popular Guide* appeared here. It is useful for gardeners as well as cooks and shoppers.

The Urban Farmer has some unusual daikons, including Early 40 Days, whose seed is used for spicy, pungent sprouts, and Aomarukoshin, also known as Green Chinese radish. This curious and delicious radish weighs more than a pound when mature. It is a longish cylinder in the Hong Kong markets, but the strain the Urban Farmer carries is round and flattened at the base. Both types have green skins, but the Urban Farmer's reveals a unique deep-red heart when cut; the color flares out in raylike bands through the white flesh when this daikon is sliced, making a beautiful flower effect. The more pedestrian Green Chinese radishes have green interior flesh. The Chinese use this radish almost exclusively in soups, and it is pungent, but is so striking in appearance that it has a place in crudités.

The names of daikon cultivars usually reflect the town or region where the type originated.

Growing Extraordinary Daikon
Daikon growers should prepare very deep loamy beds twenty-four to thirty inches in depth, without stones or lumps that could make the roots crooked. No fresh manure or unfinished compost should be worked in, for the

roots, like those of carrots, will fork and be hairy. Prepare soil as if for enormous carrots.

The seeds are planted three inches apart and later thinned to let the seedlings stand six to nine inches apart, depending on the cultivar. Spring daikons are sown as early as the frosts are past. Autumn types are sown in July or August for fall harvest. The cool nights improve the quality of the flesh. If these late-season daikon are sown in spring, you will probably lose the crop, for they will bolt to seed in the heat instead of putting their efforts into root development.

Harvest daikon when they are a little on the youthful side of mature.

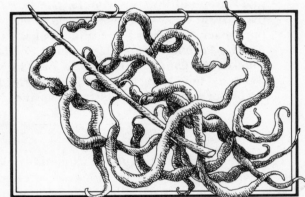

RAT-TAIL RADISH

(R. sativus var. caudatus)

This unusual and delicious radish, a native of southern Asia, produces slim, edible pods a foot or more long. They are dark green, sometimes with purple streaking. This plant is also called the serpent radish, because many of the pods curl and twist into interesting shapes. The roots of the rat-tail are inedible, thin, stringy affairs, not good for the table. The long, slender pods, on the other hand, are mild in flavor, tender, and very good to eat raw with a sprinkle of salt and lemon juice or with dips. This is a striking and delicious vegetable seldom seen in crudités. The pods can be pickled or cut and stir-fried in addition to being enjoyed fresh.

Rat-tail radishes came to England from Java around 1816, though Linnaeus knew them forty years before. They were grown in American gardens in the 1860s, but were dropped from seed catalogs later on. Even now it is difficult to find the seed. My source is Greenleaf Seeds in Conway, Massachusetts.

Growing Extraordinary Rat-tail Radishes

The rat-tail is the easiest of the radishes to grow. Plant the seed in rich, loamy soil after the frosts are gone. You need not prepare a fine-sifted or deep bed since the roots will make their way as best they can. Thin the plants to stand twelve to eighteen inches apart. Keep them weeded and watered. The green serpents develop and grow over the summer, and seventy to ninety days after the seed was sown, they should be ready. Pick them for crudités when they are no bigger than a pencil. They can be enjoyed fresh, or blanched and chilled. Larger rat-tails are good tossed into the wok and stir-fried.

TURNIP

(Brassica rapa)

Raw, fresh turnip is an excellent vegetable for crudités. It has a fine, mild flavor when properly grown and an agreeably crisp texture. The turnip is an ancient vegetable from western Asia, probably domesticated in that cradle of garden vegetables, the Mediterranean lands where so many migrating prehistoric peoples passed, lingered, and planted seeds. The turnip's "root" is botanically not a root at all, but a swollen hypocotyl, the section of the plant between the root and the stem; this is also true of beets, radishes, and rutabagas.

The Romans knew turnips well; both Pliny and Columella listed cultivars esteemed for the table. Through the ages there have been accounts of enormous turnips that astounded the neighborhood—forty-pound hulks in ancient Rome, a hundred-pounder in California in 1850. Gerard, writing in *The Herball, or generall historie of plantes* (1597,1633), had his favorite: "The small turnip grown by a village near London, called Hackney, in a sandie ground, and brought to the crosse in Cheapside by the women of that village to be solde, are the best that I ever tasted." William Rhind tells us that Laplanders were so fond of turnips they would swap a whole cheese for a single turnip, and as for the Russians, "turnips are used as fruit and eaten with avidity by all classes. In the houses of the nobility, the raw turnip cut in slices is handed about on a silver salver, with brandy, as a provocative to the more substantial meal."

Among the cultivars that Rhind mentions were the Maltese Golden turnip, of orange color, grown in India: "When quite fresh, and just before it has acquired its full consistence, it makes its appearance in the northern parts of the country with the dessert, and it is considered to be superior both in form and flavour to many fruits." The long, cylindrical French navet, with its fine-grained flesh and mild, but unique, flavor was considered the cream of the turnip crop in nineteenth-century Europe and was much grown in France and Germany.

A nineteenth-century pedant, one Dr. Desaguliers, noted by Rhind, calculated that the weight of a single turnip seed increased fifteen times its own weight every minute while the turnip was growing.

Turnips were cut into curious shapes for the pleasure of diners long before the present day. Rhind laments that the cooks of his time seemed to have lost the ability to prepare the turnip "compared with those efforts of gastronomic skill by which the ancients made it assume so many inviting forms." He tells an exemplary story:

> The king of Bithynia, in some expedition against the Scythians in the winter, and at a great distance from the sea, had a violent longing for a small fish called *aphy*—a pilchard, a herring, or an anchovy. His cook cut a turnip to the perfect imitation of its shape; then, fried in oil, salted, and well powdered with the grains of a dozen black poppies, his majesty's taste was so exquisitely deceived, that he praised the root to his guest as an excellent fish.

Vilmorin-Andrieux lists sixty-three turnip cultivars, both the long cylindrical and the flattened globe shapes, including the famous Jersey navet, "the kind which is most generally grown by the market-gardeners of Paris, so that it is rare to find the Central Market without it at any season." These pages also illustrate such turnip delights as the Jersey Lily, the bright-red Scarlet Kashmir turnip, the dark-skinned Chirk Castle Black Stone with its sugary, fine, firm flesh, and the Orange Jelly, soft and tender and slightly bitter. Orange Jelly was a great favorite in Scotland and apparently something of an acquired taste.

Surprisingly, many of these old turnips are still around. The big news-maker in recent years is the very delicious Gilfeather turnip, passed along from gardener to gardener in the town of Dummerston, Vermont, since John Gilfeather brought the seed to the area from Ireland in 1870. It is thought to be a strain of a sweet, white German turnip. The skin is rough, but the flavor of the raw Gilfeather is mild, sweet, and crunchy. In 1980 it was registered by the USDA Plant Variety and Protection Division as a unique vegetable, and seed was deposited in the National Seed Storage Laboratory in Colorado. Gardeners can buy the seed from Elysian Hills, RFD 1, Dummerston, Brattleboro, Vermont 05301.

Ohno Scarlet is a red-skinned turnip available through the Seed Savers Exchange and from Johnny's Selected Seeds. If this cultivar is pickled, the flesh is tinted red. Another red-skinned turnip is Milan Rouge from Le Jardin du Gourmet. The yellow-fleshed Golden Ball, fine-grained and of good flavor, comes from Nichols Garden Nursery, as does a fast-growing small white turnip, the Presto. Nichols also has the French black-skinned Longue de Caluire, and the very large but tender and sweet Gros Longue d'Alsace.

The old and honored Jersey Navet is around still, under the name des Vertus Marteau. Both Epicure and the Urban Farmer carry it. The flavor of this cultivar is best when the turnip is closer to forty days old rather than the sixty suggested on the packet. Purple Top White Globe is another oldie sold by many seedsmen, who also carry the popular hybrid, Tokyo Cross, which is uniform in shape, quality, and maturation date. The greens of Tokyo Cross are esteemed for the pot. Bountiful Gardens has the good old Snowball (once called Early Six Weeks) and also the old Orange Jelly.

Growing Extraordinary Turnips

Turnips are not often grown well here. And they must be at their best flavor for crudités. Once the tricks of turnip culture are learned, it is easy to grow meltingly tender, very sweet turnips that astound people who think of the turnip as a depressing, bitter mush one can't escape at Thanksgiving dinner. It is no wonder that turnips are regarded in some parts of the world as crisp, sweet fruits.

Turnips are a fast-growing, cool-season crop. They do not do well planted after the frosts have gone and let to grow in the increasing heat of summer with the bulk of the vegetables in the garden. Many turnip cultivars will bolt to seed if the weather takes a turn for the hot and dry. Turnips are ready to be pulled forty to sixty days after the seed is sown, and they can be planted either for an early summer harvest, when the main body of the garden is just getting going, or sown in summer for a fall crop. An old saying goes,

"Sow turnips wet or dry, on the twenty-fifth of July." The late-summer plantings that aim the turnips toward harvest just as the cool weather and frosts hit are superior to early-summer turnips in flavor, sweetness, and texture. The early-season turnips can hardly escape running into warm weather, and then higher rates of transpiration make the leaves draw sugar from the root. Far sweeter and crisper are the turnips grown quickly and evenly during cool fall days, pulled when they are only two or three inches in diameter. Overmature turnips (another great turnip-growing fault all too common) can be coarse, woody, and bitter.

Turnips are tolerant of most soils, though the loamy soils allow the hypocotyl to swell rapidly. Sow the seed in bands about four inches wide, or in rows. Sow thinly, and when the seedlings emerge, thin them out to stand four inches apart. Keep the turnips cool and well watered. It is important not to let them suffer drought stress, for their quality will be irretrievably diminished.

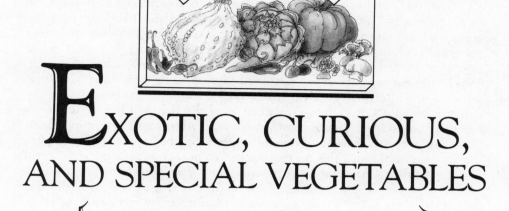

CHAPTER 3

EXOTIC, CURIOUS, AND SPECIAL VEGETABLES

Globe Artichoke / Asparagus / Tronchuda Cabbage
Cardoon / Celtuce / Chile / Jicama / Kudzu / Lotus Root
Shiitake Mushroom / Pumpkin / Rampion / Tomatillo
Wild Rice / Scorzonera / Sea Kale / Sorrel

Gourmet gardeners will not stop at carrots and tomatoes, no matter how luscious and piquant their taste, no matter how freshly picked. There are rarer birds to be caught for your horticultural and gustatory pleasure: lotus root from a tub water garden, wild rice from a brook-fed pond, watercress from the brook itself, blue corn for tortillas, tomatillos for *salsa verde*, Chinese summer melons, French cornichons for pickling, Japanese shiitake mushrooms—all can be grown in the new kitchen garden and its environs.

Occasionally, taking certain vegetables when they are very young is an unusually fine treat. André Simon writes about very young artichokes eaten whole, fresh, and uncooked (too young for the choke to have formed) with a vinaigrette sauce or only a grain of salt—"*à la croque-au-sel*"—nutty, tender little morsels. Or very tiny brussels sprouts, as they like them in France, still tightly furled, rushed from the garden to a steamer on the kitchen stove and cooked, uncovered, until barely tender, then drained and put into hot butter until they deepen in color, and finally served with a drop or two of lemon juice and a twist of the pepper mill. Okra, as it is prepared in the Middle East under the name of *bamia*, is added raw to salads in its youngest, tenderest stage, or fried quickly in hot oil.

Vegetables should be picked or pulled early in the day, while they are still cool from their night rest and before the hot sun dissipates and flattens the aromatic oils and flavors. André Simon, who, in addition to being one of the great food and wine writers of this century, was an avid gardener, wrote on the benefits of the early-morning visit to the garden: "Only they who have a vegetable garden can tell how much better a cauliflower is which was gathered in the early hours of the day, with the morning dew on it, than one picked in the afternoon after the sun has dried it up." It is this freshness, the delicate bouquets or rich, earthy aromas of the fruits of the garden only recently parted from their parent vine or stalk, that makes them incomparably superior to commercial vegetables that may be bigger and more photogenic, but stale and flat on the palate. In no restaurant can one get a platter of Silver Queen sweet corn, wrenched from the stalks ten minutes earlier, stripped of the squeaking shucks and brown-tipped silk, plunged into the boiling kettle for four minutes, then brought forth and rolled in sweet, creamy butter. The tender kernels burst between one's teeth, the sweet, buttery flavor is incomparable; and there is no substitute for it on the face of the earth. And then there are the musky, deep-fleshed cantaloupes ripened on the vine until the apricot-colored flesh is almost translucent, when their aroma and heavy weight pull the gardener to his knees on the straw of the melon bed. One of the melons is slipped off the vine, the knife pressed into the fragrant meat, and the seeds allowed to spill out onto the ground. The gardener enjoys it there in the sunshine, the juice running down his chin, his mouth filled with the rich, fine flesh.

GLOBE ARTICHOKE

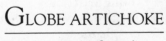

(*Cynara scolymus*)

The globe artichoke is a close relation of the cardoon. It is a perennial plant that is usually propagated by division in the spring, but the seed can also be sown, and the plants will produce edible heads in the second year. One cultivar will bear in its first season. The plant is a thick, handsome creature, growing up to five feet tall.

The artichokes of the dinner table are actually the immature flowers of the plant, which would burst into thick, thistlelike purplish-blue blossoms if they were allowed. Gardeners generally subvert the plant's intention for the sake of the fleshy bases of the individual bracts and the tender heart that lies beneath the "choke."

"No where," writes William Rhind in his *History of the Vegetable Kingdom*, "does the artichoke arrive at greater perfection than the Orkney Islands....consequent on the plentiful supply of sea weed with which the ground is annually dressed."* Many other plants thrive on a seaweed dressing, especially the delicious sea kale, and gardeners who travel to the ocean or who are well placed enough to live near it are wise to gather seaweed for the compost heap.

The globe artichoke seems not to have been known to the ancients. The first Italian reference was in the middle of the fifteenth century, and Sturtevant remarks that Ermolao Barbara "who died as late as 1493, knew of only a single plant grown as a novelty in a private garden." A century later the artichoke was being grown in France for food, introduced by Catherine de Médicis, who had an ungovernable passion for the exquisite, subtle flesh of the artichoke. Her fondness for them shocked the French court, says Waverly Root in *Food*, for the vegetable was considered to be an aphrodisiac. Root quotes an outraged older woman as writing: "'If one of us had eaten artichokes, we would have been pointed out in the street. Today young women are more froward [sic] than pages at the court.'"

Artichokes came across the Channel and into the court of Henry VIII. Rhind has picked out several references to artichokes from the Privy Purse expense books of that reign: "Paied to a servant of maister Tresorer in rewarde for bringing Archecokks to the King's grace to Yorke place, 111j*s*, iiij*d*." He adds that a treatise on growing the vegetable was written a few years later, and is Harleian Library number 645. Artichokes did not have an easy time of it in England, for late in the seventeenth century, and again in 1739, says Rhind, "most of the artichokes in England were destroyed by frost, but were replaced from France."*

By this time artichokes were the absolute rage, the most exotic and elegant of all vegetables, according to the fashions of the day, and were well on their way to becoming the symbols of total decadence, the food of rich and idle voluptuaries. Today the artichoke is still considered a luxury food.

There are several kinds of artichokes around. The big green globe artichoke, grown in tremendous quantities in California and the Breton peninsula of northern France, is the most familiar. In Provence the little purple-brown ones are well liked, and in Italy a number of cultivars are grown, including the tiny *Carciofini*, which is canned in oil and sold in specialty shops for hors d'oeuvres. Other cultivars known in Europe are the *Vert de Florence* and the Purple Venice, both of which are steamed and eaten whole when immature. Purple Globe, Creole, and *Vert de Laon* are others.

In this country one never sees seed of any but the globe artichoke. However, there are several strains of the globe around. Most common is Green Globe. A noteworthy new cultivar is *Grande Beurre*, carried by Thompson and Morgan, which will bear in its first year. J. L. Hudson has Early Green Provence, with slender, long green heads that are eaten raw with a sprinkle of salt when very young.

Artichoke seed, like apple seed, does not run true to type, so it is best to use suckers from a known parent plant. Sucker-started plants usually give a few flower buds the first season. Seed of distinct cultivars is very unlikely to be consistent.

Artichoke culture is generally restricted to warm climates where a steady supply of water is available; in this country that means California and the Deep South, for the plant is a perennial that has to winter over its first year before it can produce the edible artichoke buds. The plant is huge and striking in appearance, like an eighteenth-century colored engraving of some exotic flora. Gardeners in the North must go to great lengths to grow fresh artichokes at home, but many have done so successfully by growing them in a sheltered environment and protecting the roots and sometimes the entire plant over the winter; by growing an early cultivar such as *Grande Beurre* as an annual for the sake of a few first-year buds; or by planting the artichokes in large tubs that can be wheeled into the greenhouse or solarium in winter.

Ideal for the artichoke is a rich and fertile bed of sandy loam. Drainage in such soil is good, an important factor with the artichoke, for standing water rots the crowns. Nevertheless, the plants need plenty of water on a regular schedule, and it is not possible to depend on natural rainfall if you want quality artichokes, not even if you live in the Orkneys.

California gardeners work up their artichoke beds in sequence; one-, two-, three- and four-year-old plants are bedded in age groups, with a nearby sucker bed to supply fresh stock for the vacancies left by retiring four-year-old plants as the succession of young, vigorous plants comes along. Plants can be started from seed as well as suckers.

Seed should be sown in the hotbed six weeks before the spring frosts end, and after hardening them off for a week or ten days, the little plants are transplanted into the nursery bed. Because artichoke seed is so variable, mark the best plants (earliest buds, best flavor, longest production span, resistance to cold) and take suckers from these winners later on. Less desirable plants can be pulled up and thrown onto the compost heap.

Sucker stock may come from seed-started plants in the home garden or from nurseries. If you want a specific cultivar, try to find sucker stock from known parents.

Artichoke bud sizes will vary; buds may be only two inches across in a hostile climate and a whopping five inches in California gardens. The buds are picked before the scales begin to unfold, or one risks toughness and poor flavor.

Artichoke plants can withstand a light frost, but they are damaged when the temperature drops down around 27 degrees F. The roots may survive in places where winter *air* temperatures go down to 15 degrees F, *if* they are protected by a heavy twelve-inch mulch that stays in place until a few weeks before the spring frosts end. Areas such as New England, Minnesota, and most of Canada, where winter temperatures are truly severe, simply cannot support artichoke roots unless conditions are somehow exceptional. *If* the microclimate is superior and well protected, *if* there is early snow cover, *if* the roots are heavily mulched, they might make it through an occasional winter. It is a better risk to take suckers from a good, early-bearing parent plant after the first frosts, trim back the plant to within an inch of the crown, and then store both crowns and suckers in a cool, dry cellar (35 to 45 degrees f) over the winter. These can be planted out in spring. While some of the material is inevitably lost, some will grow and fruit the next summer. This is a tricky and laborious way to keep an artichoke bed going, but some northern gardeners think it worth the trouble.

A mature artichoke plant can produce up to twenty suckers. Where the parent plant can winter over, gardeners take all but five or six suckers for propagation when the suckers are about a foot high. In those northern gardens where the parent plants haven't a prayer of making it through the winter, you can take all the suckers and store them over the winter, or, as mentioned above, take both suckers and crowns to safe winter storage.

Artichokes make a stunning and dramatic plant in the ornamental border if you have room. Kate Rogers Gessert, whose fine book, *The Beautiful Food Garden*, has never received the attention it deserves, advises:

> A row of artichokes makes a great summer hedge or garden space divider; the plants are striking in front of a dark wall or evergreen hedge.

A massed bed of artichokes is too bulky in most gardens. A single plant in a tub makes a space-consuming but handsome focal point for a patio.

The grey-green foliage of cardoon, sage, dusty miller, olive, and Russian olive matches those of artichoke.

ASPARAGUS

(*Asparagus officinalis*)

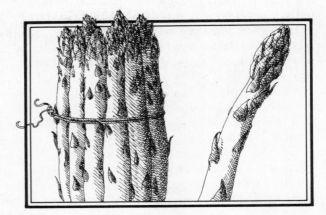

Our hardy perennial domestic asparagus is a refined form of the *A. officinalis* that is native to the sandy soils of the seacoast and riverbanks of Europe, North Africa and Asia. Sturtevant says, "In the southern parts of Russia and Poland, the waste steppes are covered with this plant." For the home gardener, asparagus is the grand treat of springtime, and over and over again our magazines of fine cuisine feature this handsome delicacy in spring issues. Some advanced gardeners can force autumn asparagus if they live in the right climate. California's Imperial Valley growers cater to the luxury market with such out-of-season asparagus. Very fine white asparagus is still grown in Belgium and France, as well as in Germany, particularly in the region north of Lake Constance. In the asparagus season in Germany, local restaurants and hotels offer menus featuring the huge blanched stalks of this specialty asparagus. One inn lists sixty-six asparagus delights on its menu in the season.

The domesticated asparagus was well known to Roman gardeners, although, according to Cato, who gives full directions on how to grow the succulent spears, the seed they used was gathered from the wild. Only when we come to the time of Columella, in the first century A.D., more than two hundred years after Cato wrote, do we see instructions for transplanting rootstocks from the nursery bed into the producing bed. Pliny, too, wrote on asparagus, describing it as the most pampered plant in the garden. It still is. According to Pliny, the best wild asparagus grew on the island of Nisida, off the Campanian coast, and he mentioned the outstanding asparagus grown at Ravenna, where the soil is sandy. This asparagus was grown in heavily manured beds and produced stalks of such size that three of them weighed a pound.

The Romans thought asparagus a great delicacy and gave the vegetable a lasting reputation as a gourmet treat. Caesar Augustus was particularly fond of it. Barbara Norman, in her delightful *Tales of the Table*, describes an opulent feast given for *pontifex maximus* Metellus on his return to Rome after a year on duty in Spain; the menu included asparagus among the twenty-six dishes—which also featured such treats as sea urchins, thrushes, a basin of clams, dog cockles (a kind of shellfish), sea nettles, figpeckers, wild-boar kidneys, sow udders, wild-boar testicles, roasted hare and fowls, a rack of boar, and boiled duck.

The famous book of recipes *De Re Coquinaria*—which dates roughly to the second century A.D. and is attributed to that most devoted of gourmets, Marcus Gavius Apicius, who squandered an immense fortune on lavish feasts and rare delicacies, and then, rather than suffer the stringencies of a reduced diet when his money was gone, killed himself—contains a Roman recipe for *Asparagus Patina*. It sounds something like a modern Italian *frittata*:

> Put in the mortar asparagus tips, pound, add wine, pass through the sieve. Pound pepper, lovage, fresh coriander, savory, onion, wine, *liquamen*, and oil. Put puree and spices into a greased shallow pan, and if you wish, break eggs over it when it is on the fire, so that the mixture sets. Sprinkle finely ground pepper over it and serve.*

During the long ages that followed the collapse of the high-living Roman Empire, asparagus faded back to its wild state in sandy waste ground until the sixteenth century. Suddenly, it was rediscovered, and by the seventeenth century, it had become, along with globe artichokes, the most fashionable vegetable of the period. Once again asparagus reclined on silver dishes. Royalty and nobility strove to have the expensive luxury on their tables. Jean de la Quininie, the head gardener of Louis XIV, forced asparagus in hotbeds all through the year. Asparagus retained its exalted position, and by the nineteenth century in Belgium and France, very large, very white, meltingly tender asparagus became the symbol of the decadent life

---

*Quoted in Barbara Norman, *Tales of the Table* (Englewood Cliffs: Prentice-Hall, Inc., 1972) p. 181.

de luxe, and the spears were an extremely important crop in the environs of Paris, particularly at Argenteuil, where skilled growers perfected the art of growing these big, blanched beauties of exquisite flavor. Only in the past few decades has the public taste turned from the voluptuous white asparagus to very green spears that look health-giving and nutritious. The shift is part of the general move toward fresh green vegetables rather than the bland, effete blanched produce so popular in the past, and the appearance of asparagus, celery, endive and chicory, lettuces, and other green foods has changed back to its natural viridian.

Children are always amazed at the transformation of thick spears of asparagus to an airy mass of green feathers. William Rhind describes the dramatic metamorphosis almost poetically:

> The branches, which lie so thick together, safe and well-protected under their scaly leaves, soon begin to be developed, and are drawn out until the whole plant, with its numerous thread-like leaves, assumes . . . the character of a larch tree, having its miniature parts more light and elegant, and the color of a more lively green.

Rhind also reminds us, somewhat disquietingly, that "one who eats a head of asparagus eats in that little space the rudiments of many hundreds of branches and many thousands of leaves."*

One often finds on old properties an asparagus bed that has reverted to the wild, or is filled with the pencil-thin sucker shoots called spruce. The flavor of these little shoots is very good in asparagus soups and omelets, so it is worthwhile to carry a jackknife and a bandanna in your pocket when you walk out in the spring fields. I have come home many times with a dozen of these little spears. Do not bother with the asparagus that grows alongside the road if there is much volume of traffic—the lead in the exhaust fumes can make toxic.

There are enough asparagus culinary masterpieces to fill a set of encyclopedias, but the subtle flavor of the spears is at its best when they are brought in fresh from the garden bed, cooked upright in a deep asparagus cooker so that the thick stems become tender and the steamed heads do not disintegrate, then served in a fine china plate with melted butter or hollandaise. Charles H. Baker, Jr., author of one of the most entertaining cookbooks ever written, *The Gentleman's Companion, or Around the World with Knife, Fork and Spoon* (1939, 1946), had a word or two to say about "ASPARAGUS after the ROMAN MANNER, Advocated for the Sunday Morning Breakfast":

One morning, with our moral visibility somewhat withered on the vine from doing as the Romans do, we wondered what things interesting might be kitchened for breakfast. And this gem Luigi suggested asparagus, first verbally, then at our evident poor Italian, not too clearly through a rough pencil sketch—more starkly phallic than anything vegetable.

He gives the recipe for eggs shirred in sour cream and served up with asparagus browned in garlic-scented olive oil, the whole sprinkled with Parmesan cheese and run under the broiler until bubbling hot.

The cultivars most prized by European gastronomes of the nineteenth century were Giant Argenteuil; Belgian, or Maline, asparagus (similar to the Giant Dutch Purple), which was a thick, pale stalk with a rose-red head; and Lauris, an improved type of green English asparagus developed in the south of France.

In this country, asparagus cultivars have been dominated for years by Mary Washington, still an excellent cultivar that grows dependably in many climates. But new strains are beginning to appear in our catalogs, many of them hybrids, most of them descendants of Mary Washington. Thompson and Morgan carry one-year-old crowns of Lorella, a new French cultivar with very thick stems and heavy yields. Jersey Centennial is one of the new hybrids, and it is still in scarce supply. It grows well in northern states. The University of New Hampshire developed Emerald, a vigorous, pure-green stalk with no trace of purple in the head; it is hardy in the North. From the University of California come a number of controlled crosses that have been cloned into male and female. The male plants have up to 50 percent larger yields and no seedling sprouts. Two of these cultivars are UC 157 and UC 72, both descended from Mary Washington.

In choosing new cultivars of asparagus, keep in mind that certain strains do best in fairly specific environments. A West Coast asparagus may be a failure in Massachusetts. Local experiment stations test-grow the new cultivars as a matter of course to see what does well where; check with one near you before going to the trouble of putting in a whole bed of untried asparagus cultivars.

Asparagus beds can be started with seed or with crowns. There is much to be said for planting seed—not only is the cost ten times less, but the harvests can be up to 40 percent heavier in the first five years of production. Of course, there will be nothing to eat until the third year! And there are difficulties for the unwary buyer of asparagus seed. A great deal of the seed—most of it—is collected on a large scale from fields of plants of mixed quality. Harris Seeds in Rochester, New York, is one of the few companies that harvests asparagus seed selectively from its New Jersey fields. Moreover, western-grown seed of asparagus cultivars is usually less hardy and less resistant to asparagus rust disease than is eastern-grown seed of the same cultivar. Don't hesitate to ask questions of a seed company before you buy— gardeners have a right to know what they are buying, and an asparagus bed is a big undertaking of labor. You expect your asparagus bed to flourish for at least ten years (some have produced for half a century), and you want to start out with "the right stuff."

Asparagus is at home in sandy or light loamy soils and likes a pH of about 6.5. Heavy soils should be amended. Most gardeners go hog-wild with manure and compost and soil conditioners in the asparagus bed as though they were dealing with the heaviest feeders in the plant kingdom. Asparagus will thrive with less preferential treatment. More important than rich soil is superlative drainage.

To plant crowns, dig a trench twelve inches wide and six inches deep the length of the bed. Shallower plantings make thinner, tougher spears, and deeper plantings slow shoot emergence. The trenches (if you have more than one) should be spaced four to five feet apart. The asparagus crowns will spread vigorously and expand through the soil on most sides of the trench over the years.

An inch or so of good, well-rotted compost is spread at the bottom of the trench, and the crowns set in place about eighteen inches apart. Healthy one-year-old crowns are best. Don't think old crowns will give you asparagus any faster; they won't, and the transplant shock to such mature plants will set them back considerably.

Cover the crowns with two or three inches of soil, patting it firmly into place to prevent air pockets from forming around the roots. As the spears emerge in coming weeks, add more soil, until by the end of the summer the trench is slightly mounded for good rain runoff. The first year, the bed is often mulched after the spears are up, to keep weeds down and to control erosion. Do not cut any of the spears that come up in this first season. The roots need to establish themselves very solidly, and cutting spears puts great stress on the young plants. Keep the bed weeded and watered throughout the summer.

In the second season you can allow yourself the treat of harvesting some of the spears for two or three weeks, but then you must control yourself and let the plants continue to build up underground strength. Do not take more than 10 percent of the spears.

By the third year you have earned a long harvest, six to eight weeks of delicious asparagus. You can figure about a pound of asparagus will be harvested from each foot of length in the trench; that is, a fifty-foot trench will give you about fifty pounds of splendid spears each year.

It is possible to freeze asparagus, and many gardeners do, but others think it so inferior to the fresh that they do not bother. My next-door neighbors, who are fanciers of fresh, fresh, fresh asparagus, cut the spears and walk swiftly to the kitchen, where the water is already boiling.

If you wish to start the bed from seed, things are a little more complicated. Asparagus seed has a thick, hard coat, and it is very slow to germinate, especially when temperatures are below 75 degrees F. Germination can be speeded up when the seeds are soaked for three or four days in warm (80 degree F) water, then planted in *warm soil*. The way to tell the temperature of the soil is not to guess but to use a soil thermometer. Cold soils can be warmed up with sheets of clear plastic spread over the ground a week or so before planting. You may wish to keep the plastic loosely in place after the asparagus seed is sown if the temperatures are uncertain.

An old-fashioned way to start asparagus was to prepare a nursery bed for the seeds, which were sown thinly three or four inches apart in rows twenty inches apart. The rich beds, made up with liberal amounts of organic material, were kept weeded, watered, and tended throughout the first season. The next spring the gardener selected the biggest and strongest crowns from the nursery bed and planted them in the trench of the permanent bed as described above.

Today things are done rather differently. Seed is sown fairly thickly—two or three inches apart in the row, two or three rows within the foot-wide trench—directly in the permanent bed trench. The three-row planting is a high-yield procedure. Although this central row will play out in a few years, the yields are considerably higher during that period than if only two rows were set. It is a help if radish seed is sown at the same time as the asparagus seed, for the radishes will break the soil open for the slower asparagus seedlings. Don't forget that the soil in your bed must be warm before sowing.

Once the seeds are sown, an inch or two of soil is put over them. As the spears emerge, soil is added until the trench is mounded slightly. Many gardeners mulch a seedling bed as soon as spears emerge in order to check weeds. Salt-marsh hay is ideal, if you can get it. There is still a lot of hand weeding to be done over the summer, but keep at it and remind yourself of the pleasures to come.

The next year only a minimal crop is taken—if any. But by the third year you should be awash in asparagus. After a year or two this heavily planted bed will start to thin out as the central row is starved out, but, for years to come there will still be more asparagus than if you had started out with crowns.

TRONCHUDA CABBAGE

(*Brassica oleracea*, *Tronchuda* group)

Tronchuda kale, Portuguese kale, Tronchuda cabbage, and Portuguese cabbage are all low-growing, loose-leaved plants resembling cabbages that have been stretched on the rack until their stems have elongated. The stalks and midribs of Tronchuda cabbage are the desirable part of the plant, very tender, juicy, crisp, and meaty.

Tronchuda cabbage is a great favorite in Portugal, where many cultivars—*Penca de Chaves*, *Penca de Mirandela*, *Couve Gloria de Portugal*, *Couve Penca de Pavoa*, and others—are grown, especially in the mountains, where the cool, short growing season is well suited to *Brassicae*.

Tronchuda cabbage can take moderate frosts, and the early light frosts of autumn give the thick stems a sweeter, nuttier savor. The stems are used in many Portuguese dishes, particularly in company with the hot and highly spiced chorizo. Sometimes the parboiled, drained stalks are sautéed in olive oil after they are cut into convenient pieces. The hearty, savory cuisine of Portugal is based on the cabbage, and *sopa de couve*, as travelers to that country know, can be found on most menus. It is a rich, coriander-flavored mélange of tronchuda cabbage, chicken, chorizo, beef, potatoes, carrots, and turnips. The vegetables are often served heaped on a bed of rice, with the strained broth brought to the table as a preliminary soup course.

Couve tronchuda is a hardy plant that can stand frost quite well, and even needs it to bring out the full flavor. The plants are easy of culture as long as they are kept cool and moist. There are both curly- and smooth-leaved cultivars. Tronchuda is grown like other cabbages and is also prey to their afflictions. Seed may either be started inside and set out in early spring or sown directly in the bed in very early spring. The plants are thinned or transplanted to a distance of twelve inches. As the plant matures, the outer leaves are used first, and the thick, fleshy stalks may replace asparagus in any recipe. At the end of the season, the heads, which have had most of their stalks removed, are finally used in an autumn soup or any good cabbage recipe.

The only suppliers I have found for seed of tronchuda cabbage are Redwood City and Le Jardin du Gourmet.

CARDOON

**(Cynara
cardunculus)**

This massive plant is one of eleven species of perennial, thistlelike plants native to the Canary Islands and Mediterranean countries. Cardoon, and its cousin, the globe artichoke, have found a place in the gardens of lovers of unusual vegetables.

Cardoon grows six to eight feet tall and has big rosettes of spiny, gray-green leaves and purple thistle flowers. The root is edible, as are the thick, solid and tender leaf stalks. Many gardeners grow it for its striking ornamental appearance. The more decorative types with their deeply cut leaves are not as good for culinary uses. In autumn the big, crisp leafstalks must be blanched, like endive or the older types of celery, before they are good.

Cardoons were enjoyed by prehistoric people, and some plant historians think it may have been the first plant cultivated by humans, for cardoon seeds dating back thirty thousand years have been found. In Italy and France's Mediterranean littoral, the cardoon is still very much fancied, and a number of regional cultivars are grown for an appreciative market. The flavor, like that of endive, witloof chicory, rocket, and certain other European vegetable delicacies, is something of an acquired taste, for the nutty, subtle bitterness is strange to North American palates, which have been ruined by the belief that only the sweet is good.

The Romans were mad about cardoons, and Pliny tells us that cardoon brought the highest price of any vegetable in the marketplace. Although cardoons were highly regarded as a delicious esculent in most of Europe throughout the centuries, they never became very much liked in England, though they were planted there from the seventeenth century. M'Mahon lists cardoon in his 1806 survey of plants grown in America, commenting, "It has been a long time used for culinary purposes, such as for salads, soups and stewing." Cardoon was generally available to gardeners through most nineteenth-century catalogs of seeds.

Vilmorin-Andrieux lists only five cardoon cultivars in the 1880s, though many were known in Italy, Spain, Greece, North Africa, and the south of France. Prickly Tours Cardoon was the number-one best-seller around Paris and Tours, despite its smaller size and abundant sharp spines. A nonspiny type from the Mediterranean seacoast was the Long Spanish. Artichoke-leaved cardoons were spine-free, and a specialty of the growers in Lyons. Smooth Solid and Red Stem were other cultivars.

A few of the old cardoons are still around today. Spineless Spanish is a fast-growing plant that comes early to maturity. The French lead the garden field with several commercial cultivars—Marseilles, Improved White, and the old Cardoon de Tours with its thick, succulent stalks. Tours still has disagreeable spines. The Paris cardoon is one of the best-flavored cardoons around. J. L. Hudson and Nichols Garden Nursery both carry a spineless type of cardoon, Ivory White Smooth. Redwood City and Le Jardin du Gourmet both carry an unnamed cardoon cultivar.

The cardoon takes a bit of understanding in the kitchen. The plant is cut at ground level in the garden and stripped of any tough and wilted or yellowed outer stalks. The tender inner stalks are separated, just as one pulls apart a bunch of celery. Any tough strings are pulled away either now or after cooking. The stalks are rubbed over with a cut lemon as soon as possible to keep them from discoloring; the same goal is achieved by dropping them into a bowl of cold water after they are cut up.

Now the stalks are cut into pieces three to five inches long, and these sections are cooked in salted water or a *court-bouillon blanc* intended for vegetables that discolor. The vessel in which cardoons are cooked much be stainless steel or unchipped emanel, for any contact with corrosive metal will darken the vegetable. The pieces are cooked until tender, then drained and dried before proceeding to any of the dozens of ways the cardoon is glorified—with butter, cream, or fines herbes; fried; simmered in a casserole with beef marrow; cooked Milanese style with Parmesan cheese; glazed with Mornay sauce; dribbled with brown butter; or, *à la Piedmontèse*, sautéed with garlic, olive oil, diced anchovies, and truffles! An excellent and elegant vegetable, this cardoon.

In cold climates cardoons are started from seed indoors, eight to ten weeks before the last frosts. They are hardened off in a cold frame or cloched row for ten days or so before they are transplanted into the garden. In the South and in California, cardoon seed is sown directly in the garden in well-prepared, enriched beds. The seed is usually planted in clusters every foot or so, to be thinned out later so that the plants stand three feet apart. Cardoons grow to be big, lusty plants, so place them where they will not shade other plants that need sunlight. Sometimes it is advantageous to plant them to the west of the lettuce bed; the lettuces benefit from the cooler environment.

The soil for cardoons should be very rich with manure and compost, well drained, and of nearly a neutral pH. Composted poplar leaves make organic material that has an almost neutral pH. Cardoons will not tolerate acidic soil. The plants must be regularly watered or the edible stalks will be tough, hollow, and bitter. They are sensitive to drought and should be deeply watered every week or ten days, or more often if the situation demands it. A thick mulch helps hold moisture.

You can start harvesting the thick, meaty stalks when the plant is only a foot or so tall. Older and bigger cardoons will have woody, inedible outer stalks, but the inner stalks will be tender and delicious. Some cultivars are self-blanching, but others need help.

To blanch a cardoon, tie the stems up neatly, or set a dark-box over the plant. Earthing up does a good job of blanching and insulates the plant from summer heat damage, but you can only mound earth a little way up the plants unless you grow them in trenches! It is not a good idea to wrap up the cardoon in paper, for the internal heat can spoil the stalks. Never wrap cardoons, or any other plant, in newspaper or brown paper for blanching as some garden writers suggest; these materials will spoil the flavor completely. Wrapping green tomatoes in newspaper for cellar ripening is an equally ruinous practice unless you really enjoy kerosene-flavored tomatoes.

If you are fortunate enough to have a root cellar, you can store some of your cardoons here as the severe frosts of late autumn approach. Wrap them in freezer paper and lay them on their sides in a cool, dark place. They hold fresh and firm for some weeks.

CELTUCE

(*Lactuca sativa* var. *asparagina*)

This delicious and unusual hardy annual is also called stem lettuce. It has been grown in northern China for centuries and only came to North America in the 1940s. One story has it that a seed company introduced it here under the name of celtuce (a lettuce with a celerylike form) in 1942. Another story says that an American missionary sent home some seed from western China around 1940. The august *Hortus Third*, a comprehensive dictionary of 20,397 species of plants cultivated in North America, does not list celtuce, though several of our seedsmen now offer it, including Nichols Garden Nursery, Thompson and Morgan, William Dam, and Burpee.

The celtuce stem grows up to fifteen inches tall and is as large around as the giant leeks. The stem looks like a tiny coconut palm tree in texture with red-toned leaf scars up and down the length. The thin but rather tough leaves resemble narrowed lettuce leaves, and they have a strong, somewhat bitter lettucey taste. The leaves must be used when they are still young, before they get too bitter to be palatable. They are best torn into pieces and added to mixed salads with a preponderance of milder leafage.

The leaves are minor parts of the celtuce. It is the heart of the stem that is the choice morsel and the reason we grow the plant. The stem is cut and washed when it is about one inch in diameter, and the leaves are stripped off and set aside for salad or other use. The outer layer of the stem is somewhat fibrous and tough and contains tubes of bitter sap. This outer layer is peeled away to expose the tender, very juicy and crisp greenish-white pith. This is a most pleasing and unique vegetable in the *crudité* arrangement. It can be cut into matchsticks or other shapes, including brushes.

The crunchy, succulent pith can be sliced and mixed with any salad dressing or added to a mixed salad—perhaps just a few buttery leaves of the tenderest Bibb lettuce, so that its mild flavor can be fully appreciated. In China it is often stir-fried with chicken and pork dishes. It can be steamed and served like asparagus or deep fried until light brown and crunchy. The Chinese most often pickle stem lettuce, and one can find it in oriental specialty food stores and restaurants under the name "Shanghai pickles."

Growing celtuce is not difficult, for the plant is tolerant of soil. It does like a prepared bed conditioned with aged manure. Cool weather lets it mature to a high level of quality. Southern gardeners can start plants and set them out in the garden as early as February. Northern gardeners seed directly into the permanent bed as soon as the soil can be worked. An autumn crop is the result of late-summer seeding. Plants are thinned to stand about eighteen inches from each other. Water supply should be regular, and mulch does a lot to hold the moisture in the soil. Some gardeners side-dress the celtuce midway through the season with a good compost or a shot of manure tea.

CHILE

(Capsicum annuum)

In the Southwest and Mexico, hot chile is not a spice but a food. An average family in New Mexico consumes four hundred to five hundred pounds of fresh chile a year in the form of chiles rellenos and hot salsa, as an accompaniment to beans, in salads, in confections and pies, *con carne*, roasted and peeled as a side dish, pickled, in omelets, and even in green chile pie.

Capsicum annuum is one of five major chile species, and in this group are scores of delicious and fiery hot chile cultivars as well as the familiar sweet bell peppers, pimiento types for stuffing olives, and the shiny red patent-leather paprika peppers, mild and sweet and piquant.

The wonderful hot chiles that grow throughout Mexico, the Southwest, and South America include many commercial types from the breeders, such as Numex Big Jim, Española, Sandia, and others. Local breeds are known all through the chile regions, many restricted to a certain village or even a single family for generations. In the Southwest, Española and Chimayo Beauty are such regional types. There are purple chiles from the Andes; mulatto chiles, which are a rich chocolate brown when mature; the tiny but incendiary "bird" peppers from the Caribbean; the firm and thick and aromatic Mexican jalapeño in a diversity of cultivars.

The ancient Aztecs usd chile not only as a food but to punish naughty children. The angry parents would throw a few chile pods on the fire and hold the miscreant in the smoke, which stung the eyes and made each breath fiery torture. In the Caribbean, certain Indian tribes given to cannibalism were known to delight in torturing their victims for some days before the feast by rubbing chiles into cuts and wounds. One unsympathetic historian suggests that they may have been seasoning the main dish as well as amusing themselves with the victim's anguish.

Chiles are most frequently used when they are green, for stuffing and for sauces. They are picked when they are mature, but before they start to turn red, then roasted over coals until the skin blisters and blackens a little. They are set aside to cool a little and then peeled. They can be used at once in hundreds of fine regional dishes, or else frozen for later use. Cooks of the Southwest sometimes roast the chiles and then freeze them, only peeling the skins off when they are defrosted and ready for the dish. It is quite possible to roast chiles in a broiler or over a gas ring in an apartment, but be sure to open the windows for good ventilation. I once did eighty pounds of chile this way on a cold November day in Vermont and found the stinging fumes quite painful and unpleasant to breathe.

Chile peppers will grow and generally mature anywhere one can grow corn, but away from their natural home in the Southwest or tropical America, they will not develop the fierce heat nor the rich flavors natural to their kind. Travelers to the Southwest who are fortunate enough to visit during the chile harvest time (August through October) can come away with boxes and bags of this superb vegetable.

Chiles are grown in fertile, well-drained soils. They may be started inside in soil blocks, then hardened off and transplanted into the garden after all danger of frost has passed. Since they are perennials, chile peppers can also be grown in pots indoors, but hardly in quantity, for each plant can take up considerable room, twice as much as the most robust bell pepper plant. Regular watering during the summer is important; chiles cannot take water stress. Neither do they like fertilizer rich in nitrogen. Too much nitrogen causes blossom drop.

Almost all of our seed catalogs offer a few of the chile peppers, for there is a nationwide taste for southwestern cuisine, and because the cuisines of Thailand, Indonesia, Vietnam, India, and other Asian countries use dozens of the chile cultivars extensively. Some of these Pacific chiles are among the hottest known.

Horticultural Enterprises of Dallas, Texas, carries a very good selection of chile peppers, and Plants of the Southwest has the seed of several local chiles, impossible to get from any other source. Quite a few of the Seed Savers members specialize in hot chiles and grow some of the most unusual cultivars—a large hot bell fom Changee, China; a Peruvian *aji*; the tiny Bird's Eye; the Brazilian, the Chipotle, Cuban Clusters, several Italian types, Szechwan Number Two, Tabasco, and many more. Redwood City and J. L. Hudson often have unusual offerings in the chile line, and both buy seed from native collectors in South America, who supply them with unusual and rare cultivars. A recent card from Redwood City lists Cascabel, Chilacate, Guijillo, Mirasol, and Mulata in addition to their regular types. Most of these are not obtainable from other sources in this country.

Chile lovers should not bother with jalapeño seed offered in American seed catalogs unless they know for sure that it is one of the fragrant, flavorful Mexican jalapeños (there are a dozen subtypes), for the two jalapeños developed in America are hot enough, but lack the good flavors of the Mexican cultivars.

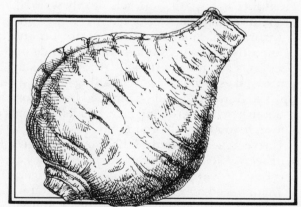

JICAMA

(Pachyrhizus erosus)

This narrow-necked, fat-bottomed root vegetable is a native of tropical America, though it has been known and used in Southeast Asia since the Spaniards introduced it to the Philippines in the seventeenth century. It is a favorite vegetable in Mexican cuisine, traditionally peeled and sliced and eaten raw with a hot chile dip, a small dish of salt, and wedges of fresh lime. In restaurants it is sometimes served in slices for scooping up guacamole. Jicama can be cut julienne and added to salads uncooked, where its crisp, sweet flesh provides a nice crunch.

Jicama is treated much like a potato when it is cooked; it can be creamed, mashed, fried, baked, steamed, or braised in any way the more familiar tuber is used. Cantonese Chinese cooks use jicama stir-fried with shrimp, black beans, and garlic. The flavor and texture are very similar to fresh water chestnut, and far superior to the canned version of that crunchy vegetable. Jicama can be used instead of water chestnut in any recipe.

Jicama is a tropical annual vine that can attain lengths of up to twenty-five feet. In some areas it is called the yam bean. The leaves are large and heart-shaped, and in season the plant is covered with showy violet and purple flower spikes. These flowers, and the seeds they form, are *poisonous*, for they contain rotenone, which is used as a native fish poison in parts of South America and as a powerful insecticide in agriculture and gardening.

Jicama needs a long, warm growing season and rich, loamy soil. In Mexico and California the plant grows for eight or nine months before the delicious roots are harvested, but it can be grown in the South and along the warmer coastal regions as far north as southern New England in as few as four months if the gardener is satisfied with smaller roots. The roots, though petite, will be as sweet and good as the large ones of long-season gardens. The gardener who attempts to grow jicama in a short period should take great care to have the soil rich, deeply worked, light, and friable, with good amounts of potassium worked in.

Jicama seed should be soaked or presprouted before sowing in soil blocks or directly in the bed. It cannot go outside until *all* danger of frost is past. Seedlings should be set eight to ten inches apart. Some sort of support— fence, stakes, arbor, or porch railing—should be provided to hold the vines up. The flowers should be pinched back in order to force the plants to put their energy into growing larger roots. Jicamas can be grown in the greenhouse, if you have the room.

Harvest the roots in the fall as soon as the first light frosts strike. The roots will keep well in cold storage for weeks. They can be stored in the root cellar, or peeled, covered, and stored in the refrigerator.

Jicama seed may be ordered through Redwood City, Horticultural Enterprises, Nichols Garden Nursery, or Le Marché.

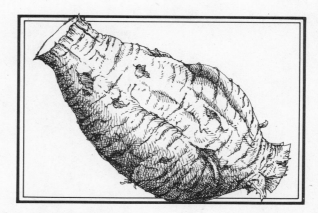

KUDZU

(*Pueraria lobata*)

Kudzu has had a tremendous amount of bad press as the vine that threatens to strangle the South. It was imported here originally from the Orient as a nutritious cattle-fodder crop and as an effective cover crop that halted erosion. Alas, the plant quickly escaped cultivation and now grows in writhing green festoons on the ground, on telephone poles, on trees, houses, farm equipment at rest, and on slow walkers. It is a very beautiful plant and has undoubtedly kept billions of tons of southern soil in place, but most southerners are heartily sick of it. It is hardy all the way up to zone 5, and northern train travelers going down the east coast will mark its luxuriant form from Philadelphia on south.

Kudzu is propagated by division, seeds, and cuttings, and it grows so enthusiastically that it has earned the name of "rampant weed." What is less known about kudzu is that the root is edible and yields a sweet starch that may be of considerable interest to cooks who want to duplicate authentic Chinese dishes.

Kudzu root is very large, up to two feet in length, and looks not unlike a giant, rough-skinned yam. The flesh is white. The root is also very, very tough and hard to cut. A sharp cleaver helps. Most of the commercial kudzu crop is processed to make a vegetable starch that is used as a sauce and soup thickener. However, the fresh root plays an important role in traditional Cantonese cooking, and if kudzu grows in your area, you might like to try using it in the kitchen.

In China the root is sliced, peeled, then coarsely chopped. It is put to boil in soup stock along with pork, beef, or chicken bones for several hours. The stock that results is thickened and remarkably sweet, thanks to the kudzu. Many traditional sweet-and-sour dishes depend on kudzu root for a translucent, subtly sweet sauce instead of the cane sugar and cornstarch procedure.

J. L. Hudson and Park Seeds both carry kudzu seed.

Lotus root

(*Nelumbo nucifera*)

Fresh lotus root is an oriental delicacy with a mild, sweet flavor and crisp texture. It is almost impossible to buy in this country except in cans, a poor substitute for the real thing. In oriental cooking, lotus root is used in soups or braised with pork. During the New Year celebration, lotus root, which is a symbol of rebirth because of the beautiful flower that springs from the mud-dwelling root, is used in dozens of dishes. One specialty is the whole lotus root stuffed with seasoned mung bean puree and braised with tender pieces of lean pork.

Lotus roots look like a string of bananas. The fat rhizomes, several inches in diameter and six to ten inches long, are joined by narrow necks. They are hard to the touch and riddled with hollow channels that make lacelike decorative rounds when cut in slices.

Lotus can be grown in sunken tubs in a garden pool, or in the muddy margins of a pond or lake. A roomy situation is superior, because the root-stock can develop into a thirty-foot-long string of rhizomes in just one season. Once the plant is established in a pond, the root systems will work deeper and deeper into the mud as the cool weather comes on until they are below the frost line—which is fortunate because the roots are frost-tender. Lotus is a vigorous grower and will survive surprisingly far north. It can be grown throughout most of the northern temperate region except on the Pacific slope. Lotus may choke out other plants unless you harvest most of the rhizomes.

If you want to confine the lotus, plant a section in a half barrel or wooden tub that is then set under water in the pool or pond. A growing section is one bananalike length with an intact, undamaged, slender growing tip. Soil for growing lotus in a tub is very important. Don't waste your time digging up that black swamp muck under the impression it is rich stuff; it is usually sour, acidic material with very little nutritive quality. Instead, use the same friable, enriched loam you would for your finest garden vegetables. One part well-rotted cow manure in the bottom of the tub with three parts good soil above makes an ideal mixture. Never use fresh manure with pond plants—you will end up with a pondful of green slime. Water gardeners advise that horse and sheep manures are too rich for tubbed plants, so avoid them. The soil in the planting box should be renewed every two years.

Lotus is planted in the early spring. The root sections arrive from the dealer wrapped in damp material, and they should be planted immediately—*never* allowed to dry out. Before you set the rhizome in place, check to be sure that the slender growing tip is undamaged. Set the rhizome about an inch under the surface of the soil in the tub and allow the growing tip to extend above the surface. Weight the root down with a flat stone, but take care not to cover over the growing tip. Set the tub in the pond or pool so that the tip is covered with three or four inches of water. If you are planting directly in a pond, treat the rhizome the same way.

Some shallow ponds freeze right to the bottom in winter. If ice touches the growing point of the lotus root, the root will be killed. You can prevent this catastrophe by digging up the roots in the fall and storing the sections with the growing tips in moist soil in a very cool place, 35 to 40 degrees, throughout the winter. Protect the rhizomes from rodents, for mice are crazy about lotus root. Set out the roots again in the spring.

When you harvest your lotus root, choose only whole, unblemished sections for the kitchen. Broken rhizomes allow mud to get inside the hollow chambers and they are almost impossible to clean out again. Wash and scrub the rhizomes well with a vegetable brush. Cut off and discard the necks between the rhizomes, with their garlands of rootlets. Peel off the outer tough skin, then slice or chop the fine vegetable. It can be boiled, baked, braised, stir-fried, or deep-fried. Oriental cookbooks contain scores of ways to prepare and use lotus root.

Lotus root growing-tip sections are available from several dealers in water plants. Lilypons Water Gardens, at 1600 Hort Road, Lilypons, Maryland 21717, or 1600 Lilypons Road, P.O. Box 188, Brookshire, Texas 77423, sells lotus root. Paradise Gardens, 14 May Street, Whitman, Massachusetts 02382, sells water plants, pond suplies, and books on water gardening.

SHIITAKE MUSHROOM

(*Lentinus edodes*)

Gourmet dishes are not automatically created by the use of exotic foods, nor can the skill of the cook triumph over limp and wilted produce. The critical factor in fine cuisine is the freshness of the vegetables and fruits. Dried, frozen, cold-stored produce has revolutionized our shopping habits, housekeeping, diet, and Gross National Product, but its flavor is *always* inferior to that of freshly gathered fruits, roots, stems, stalks, buds, and flowers that have been well grown.

Mushrooms are among the most delicious of all foodstuffs, and people who are deeply interested in fine cuisine take the time to learn enough mycology to enjoy wild morels, shaggymanes, oyster mushrooms and others that they gather for themselves in search of the incomparable flavors. The rich, meaty taste of fresh morels is as unlike the bland cellophane-wrapped *Agaricus bisporus* of the supermarket as yellow Jersey cream is from ersatz "nondairy creamer."

Stellar among the tribe of edible mushrooms is the Japanese shiitake, rich, densely textured morsels thought by some to taste like a combination of lobster and hazelnuts. Dried shiitake are usually available in specialty grocery stores at thirty dollars per pound. Fresh shiitake, once enjoyed only by travelers to the Far East, are now a culinary prize within the reach of gardeners.

Shiitake mushrooms have virtues other than flavor (as if more were needed!); they have twice as much protein as an equivalent amount of the familiar supermarket button mushrooms and contain essential amino acids at levels that compare with milk and meat.

For many years it was illegal to ship live shiitake culture into the United States for fear the mushroom spore would escape cultivation and endanger native trees, telephone poles, railroad ties, and fence posts. But in 1972 the ban was lifted, and a number of shiitake lovers began experimenting with growing them on logs as professional growers do in Japan, where more than 150,000 metric tons of the delicious mushroom are harvested each year.

The traditional way of growing shiitake is to inoculate properly seasoned three-foot-long hardwood logs with the spawn and then keep them outdoors in the proper environment. The logs bear the first crop of mushrooms two to three years later and will flush twice a year for up to five or more years. One of the hazards is that the slow-growing shiitake will be overwhelmed outdoors by wild fungi, which are always present in varying degrees. California mushroom growers have found, however, that much smaller logs—as small as six inches to a foot—can be inoculated and kept inside in a controlled environment that greatly reduces the chance of wild spore takeover.

Shiitake is an easy mushroom to grow, although the procedure sounds complicated. Actually, the steps are so far apart that one needs to make notations in an engagement calendar not to forget about them. Only one inoculation is necessary for a log that will produce for years, and no odoriferous manures or damp cable-heated beds are necessary. Oak logs are the best yielders, though other hardwoods, exclusive of apple and sycamore, have produced well in USDA experiments.

The trees for shiitake logs should be cut in autumn when nutritious sugar levels are high. Saw them into convenient log lengths and dry outdoors for thirty to ninety days, or until the log's moisture content is reduced by 50 to 60 percent. Twelve three-foot logs are calculated to keep a family supplied with all the shiitake they can eat for five or six years.

One must drill holes about three-quarters of an inch in diameter several inches apart all around the log. Dowels that have been dipped in live shiitake mycelia are inserted into the holes. In Japan the logs are now stacked outside, but the California growers prefer to store them indoors in wooden or cardboard boxes packed with hardwood sawdust at temperatures between 60 and 80 degrees for four to six months, turning the boxes occasionally. At four months the logs are examined to see if there is a furry white growth on the ends, a sign that marks the stage just before the fruiting period.

The logs are soaked in water now for a day or so, then stored again, this time in a damp environment such as an earth-floored cellar for another month to six weeks. By now spring should be on the way, and as soon as freezing weather is over, the logs can be stacked outside to dry over the summer.

As soon as the first cool autumn frosts begin and temperatures start to settle into the thirties, the logs are soaked for another day and finally placed in the damp cellar again. The mushrooms need light in order to fruit; fluorescent grow-lights or even indirect window light will do. Small log sections can simply be tossed into a bucket that has a little damp sand in the bottom. The delicious mushrooms will start to appear in two or three weeks and will flush for ten days to two weeks. As soon as production drops off, return the logs to a dry place for winter storage. In the spring, after another soaking of the log, the fruiting process starts again for the spring flush.

Detailed directions and shiitake mushroom spore, as well as the spore of other highly prized culinary mushrooms, such as velvet stem, oyster mushrooms, and Black Forest mushrooms, can be ordered from the following suppliers:

Bob Harris
Mushroom People
Box 158
Inverness, California 94937

Dr. Yoo Farm
Box 290
College Park, Maryland 20740

Fungi Perfect
Box 1286
Jacksonville, Oregon 97530

Kurtzman's Mushroom Specialties
445 Vassar Avenue
Berkeley, California 94708

Far West Fungi
Box 763
Watsonville, California 95077

PUMPKIN

**(*Cucurbita
pepo*)**

The pumpkin is among the top twenty most often grown vegetables in American gardens, says a 1974 Gardens For All survey. It is a vegetable that originated in America, and as a native plant, it gets considerable attention here. Seeds have been found in pre-Columbian graves, showing the plant's antiquity. We find it amusing to see that the pumpkin sometimes appears on European lists of "unusual and exotic plants."

Pumpkins and squashes are often botanically confused in name; certain vegetables that we call squashes are really pumpkins, including the acorn, zucchini, cocozelle, scallop, and crookneck "squashes." A distinguishing characteristic that separates the pumpkins from the squashes, and is immediately recognizable by any gardener, is that pumpkins have five-ribbed stems on the fruits; true squashes have round stems, and include Hubbard, buttercup, and Boston marrows among their number. Both the pumpkins and the squashes are excellent sources of vitamin A.

The round, orange fruit that we usually think of as the real pumpkin comes in numerous cultivars for specialized purposes. The Small Sugar, or New England Pie, pumpkin is a small fruit with fine-grained flesh that is a deep orange in color. This cultivar dates back to before 1906 and remains the finest pie pumpkin we have. It makes firm, smooth-textured pies of outstanding quality.

Connecticut Field pumpkin, a pale yellowish, rather coarse-grained type, was the pumpkin the Indians were growing when the first colonists arrived in North America, and the big fruit saw them through many rough winters. The Connecticut Field pumpkin and several "squashes" were, after corn, the major food staple for both colonists and Indians. The literature is full of references to "Pompions" and "Isquontersquashes." John Josselyn wrote in his 1672 *New-Englands Rarities* of a common way of preparing pumpkin:

> [T]he Housewives' manner is to slice them when ripe and cut them into dice, and so fill a pot with them of two or three gallons, and stew them upon a gentle fire a whole day, and as they sink, they fill again with fresh Pompions, not putting liquor to them; and when it is stewed enough, it will look like bak'd Apples; this they dish, putting butter to it and a little vinegar (with some spice, as Ginger, etc.) which makes it tart like an Apple, and so serve it up to be eaten with Fish or Flesh. It provoketh Urin extremely and is very windy.*

Both Connecticut Field and the New England Pie are still around today. The Large White is another old pumpkin, around for more than a hundred

---

*Quoted in Ann Leighton, *Early American Gardens* (Boston: Houghton Mifflin Co., 1970), p. 94.

years. It is an enormous thing, said to be good for pies; it has cream-colored skin. Redwood City sells the seed from the only white-pumpkin farm in the United States, located in Manteca, California.

In recent years there has been a fervid interest in growing enormous show pumpkins, after the example of Howard Dill, a Nova Scotia pumpkin fancier who grows world-record behemoths in the quarter-ton range. Big Max falls into the giant-pumpkin category, and so does King of Mammoth. Atlantic Giant is the masterpiece developed by Dill over the years. Two more exhibition pumpkins come from Vermont Bean Seed—Big Moon and Hungarian Mammoth. These monster pumpkins are intended only to stupefy and amaze; they are no good for eating, their flesh being coarse and watery.

Kentucky Field is a good pie pumpkin, and Young's Beauty, a medium-size fruit, is moderately good for cooking purposes and big enough for decent jack-o'-lanterns. It is a top seller at roadside stands in New England.

Of interest to the cook are the recent breeding triumphs in hull-less pumpkin seed. Early efforts gave us Naked Seed and Lady Godiva (the best cultivar name I know), and the gardener who grew these pumpkins found himself with greenish seeds that had a fine nutty flavor and did not have to be shelled. Hull-less pumpkin seed is nutritious, high in unsaturated fatty acids, phosphorus, and iron. It is of distinctive and good flavor and can be toasted or enjoyed green. However, the flesh of these pumpkins was of poor quality and the size was small—everything the plant had went into the seeds. Now we have a new generation of cultivars such as Triple Treat and Trick or Treat. Both are good-size pumpkins that can be carved for Halloween, they have acceptable flesh for culinary use, and they produce hull-less seeds. Unfortunately, the seeds are smaller and thinner than Lady Godiva or Naked Seed. Cooks will continue to plant Small Sugar for pies, pumpkin soup, and fritters and, in another plot, will sow Lady Godiva for the rich and oily seeds that don't need to be shelled. J. L. Hudson, William Dam, and Vermont Bean Seed all offer one or another of the hull-less pumpkin-seed cultivars.

The pumpkins are much grown by Seed Savers members, perhaps because it is a native plant, perhaps because its size and color dominate the eye in the garden. Through the interest of these collectors such rare pumpkins and regional cultivars as these are preserved: Bloomfield, Busch Olkurbis, Naked Seed, Cheyenne Pie, Eat All Seed, Gill's Golden Pippin, Green Stripe, Idaho Gem, No Name, Pink Giant, Tarahamara Indian Pumpkin, Tuckernuck, and the Little Tennis Ball.

RAMPION

(Campanula rapunculus)

The campanulas, or bellflowers, are 300 or so species of herbs distributed throughout the northern hemisphere, but they are particularly numerous in the Caucasus, the Balkans, and Mediterranean countries. The showy flowers of the campanulas make them great favorites in borders and rock gardens.

The species *C. rapunculus*, or rampion, is still enjoyed in Europe, where the first-year roots and the basal leaves are eaten in salads. It is a biennial plant. The root is often described as having a flavor like walnuts, and it can be enjoyed raw like a radish, or boiled and then chilled, diced and served as a cold salad with mayonnaise or cream dressing. Because rampion wilts almost as soon as it is gathered, it is never found in the produce market.

Rampions are especially liked in Germany and France. Although they were known in American gardens in the early nineteenth century, interest in the plant dropped off, until today it is virtually unknown here except as a curious garden plant (probably mythical) in the Grimm Brothers' story of Rapunzel and her golden hair. Rapunzel's mother, when pregnant, yearned for a salad made of rampion when she glimpsed some very fine green clumps of the plant growing in the garden of the witch next door. She urged her husband to steal the rampion for her. On one of his moonlight excursions he was caught, and the couple had to give up their child to the witch. The baby was Rapunzel, which is the German word for rampion.

Rampion leaves grow in light-green clusters that somewhat resemble corn salad. The roots are small, like slender little carrots but with white flesh, very crisp and pleasant in taste. The seed of rampion is extraordinarily fine, "the finest of all kitchen-garden seeds," says Vilmorin-Andrieux, which estimates twenty-five thousand seeds to a gram. A pile of rampion seed looks like dust and feels like cold water if you plunge your finger into it, as I once did at a seed house. The stems of the plant are frail and delicate, so they are usually grown fairly close together for mutual support. Rampion can be grown up into zone 4.

Seed is usually sown directly in the rampion bed after the frosts have passed. Moist, sandy soil is ideal. Since the seed is so fine, it is best to mix it with a quantity of fine sand when sowing to avoid clots and clumps of thick seedlings. Do not try to cover the fine seed over with soil, but press it into place with a length of board. Watering is done with a can that has a mist rose to avoid washing the nearly invisible seed away. It is a good idea to cover the misted row or bed with a sheet of clear plastic weighted along the edges until the plants germinate, lest wind or rain shift them out of their places.

When the rampions are up, they are thinned to stand about six inches apart. A second sowing in midsummer will give a supply of leaves and roots into autumn. Rampion roots can be pulled and made into bundles in the fall, then stored in sand in a cool root cellar for some weeks.

The seed of rampion is very difficult to find here. Redwood City is my only source.

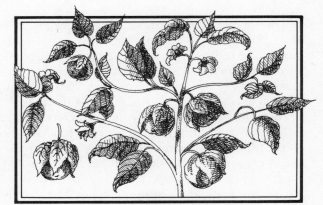

TOMATILLO

(*Physalis* spp.)

Physalis includes about eighty species of ground-cherries or husk-tomatoes, which bear yellow-greenish berries enclosed in papery husks. Some of them bear delicious edible fruits, others are better used as ornamentals. The most often used species are listed here, in an effort to sort out the catalog confusion about the differences among Cape Gooseberries, tomatillos, ground-cherries, and other popular names for these interesting plants. Each species has a number of cultivars.

Physalis ixocarpa is the *tomato verde* of Mexico, essential ingredient in the ubiquitous and delcious *salsa verde* that accompanies almost every dish in Mexican and southwestern cuisine. The most common tomatillo cultivar is Large Green, with big fruits up to two and a half inches across. This is faster and easier to dehusk than smaller cultivars, but not necessarily the best one to grow. De Milpa is a superior cultivar, bearing a purplish fruit. They keep well, but are small and more tedious to husk than Large Green. The only source of De Milpa that I have found is Redwood City, and in their catalog they say about this plant, "Only found as a semidomesticated weed in the milpas or slash-and-burn cornfields, and is much sought after. The fruits can be stored for months by pulling back the husks and stringing them like garlics."

Large Green is carried by several seed companies—Plants of the Southwest, Redwood City, J. L. Hudson, Le Marché, and others. Thompson and Morgan carry Sugar Cherry, a cultivar of Large Green.

P. peruviana is a small, yellow, edible globe with several common names—Cape gooseberry, Barbados gooseberry, poha, ground-cherry, winter cherry, cherry tomato, strawberry tomato are some of those listed in *Hortus Third*. This tender perennial has bright-yellow flowers and juicy, acidic fruits with a distinctive and delicious taste. Like the other *Physalis*, the little globes are enclosed in a papery husk like the autumn ornamental Chinese Lanterns, a nonedible relative.

Only the ripe fruits of *P. peruviana* should be eaten. They can be enjoyed whole out of the hand or stewed in light syrup for a few minutes. They make outstanding jams and jellies and are baked in pies, eaten with cream, or added to salads, stews, and meat sauces. Sometimes they are rolled in sugar and dried to make a kind of raisin. Thompson and Morgan carries a new improved cultivar of *P. peruviana*, Golden Berry, which bears large orange fruits that taste like pineapple, strawberry, and tomato combined.

P. purinosa is called strawberry tomato or dwarf Cape gooseberry, and, as the name implies, it is smaller than *P. peruviana*. This is the common husk-tomato grown in many gardens for jams and jellies. The plants are not often troubled by the pests and diseases that afflict their large cousins, the tomatoes. They do well on dry, sandy soils, but need quite a long season to mature—although catalogs tell us that they ripen "before tomatoes," hard experience teaches us that they ripen about the same time as late tomatoes. In my Vermont garden I rarely get a ripe husk-tomato except in unusually warm, sunny summers. They can be coaxed along with clear-plastic shelters and heat-holding back walls as the fall frosts approach.

Johnny's Selected Seeds carries the cultivar Goldie and has a good recipe for Husk-Cherry Pie in the catalog. Nichols Garden Nursery has an unnamed cultivar of *P. purinosa*.

General growing procedures for all *Physalis* are similar. Where the growing season is short, plants can be started inside four to six weeks before the last spring frosts. The young plants should be hardened off a week or ten days before transplanting into the garden. The bed should be warm, rich, and well-drained soil in full sun and a sheltered position where chilling breezes do not blow. Set the plants eighteen inches apart. As they ripen, the color will change from that of green marbles to yellow, orange, or purple, depending on the species you are growing. Some will burst their husks, others will stay shyly hidden until the husks are torn open. Some of the group have the habit of falling to the ground while still unripe inside the husks. They will ripen slowly but surely off the plant as long as they lie undisturbed inside the husk. Do not use any of these fruits in an unripe state.

WILD RICE

(Zizania aquatica)

Wild rice is one of the finest vegetables known, of outstanding flavor and highly nutritious. If you have a pond on your property, or access to a lakeshore, freshwater stream, or beaver pond, and live in the North, you may be able to grow wild rice. The nutty, dark grains beautifully complement wild-game entrées. In Chinese cooking, the firm, young, fresh inner shoots are stir-fried in oil with shreds of lean pork and seasoned with garlic and ginger. The shoots can also be steamed and served with melted butter or hollandaise sauce. The price of wild rice in specialty grocery shops is extremely steep, and the shoots cannot be bought for love or money.

Wild rice prefers a soft mud bottom along a freshwater stream, or on the margins of lakes or ponds, or even in a bog, as long as there is a change of water. Stagnant water will not do. Wild rice will also grow in sand.

The water should be shallow, from six inches to no more than three feet. Sunny bays and setbacks where the current is slight or where waves will not break forcefully are ideal for wild rice. Freshwater streams twenty-five to fifty miles from the sea where saline content is not too high nor tides above four feet will support wild rice, but they are not the ideal locale. Do not try to grow wild rice in salt water, in water with high alkali content, or acidic water. Marl-bottom lakes are not good places either. Rivers and tributary streams where the water level rises annually ten or more feet for several weeks will drown out wild rice.

Seed of wild rice must be fresh and moist. In nature the seed shatters out and falls into the water where it is gradually washed along the muddy margin until it is buried in soft mud. The seed grain lies dormant over winter to sprout the following spring. The plant that springs from each grain will bear a crop in the fall. Some rice grains should be allowed to fall into the water at harvest time to reseed the plot so that it will produce more rice the next year.

The gardener plants rice simply by casting the fresh seed along the muddy shore in shallow water in the autumn.

As harvesttime approaches the next fall, the gardener has to keep a sharp eye on the rice, for it shatters out very easily, and the crop can end up in the water instead of one's pantry if the grower is not there to take it when it's ready. The classic manner of harvesting wild rice is to paddle a canoe alongside the plants, bend the rice heads over the canoe floor, where a clean sheet has been spread, and strike the plants with a stick so that the grains are released.

The grains must then be dried, either on screens in a hot attic, on a shallow baking sheet in a very low oven, or in a shallow pan over low stovetop heat. After they have been parched in this manner, rub them between the palms of your hands to remove the husks. Finally, winnow the rice by placing it on a sheet again and repeatedly tossing it up in the air outdoors on a breezy day. The wind will blow the chaff, or loosened hulls, away. The heavy rice grains wil fall back onto the sheet.

When gathering wild rice, always be careful to check for ergot, the poisonous fungi (*Claviceps* spp.) associated with grain crops. Ergot is a pink or purplish color and when it hardens, it can be the shape of the rice grains or a little larger. If there is ergot in your rice stand, do *not* harvest it.

Several companies in Minnesota and Wisconsin deal in wild-rice seed and the seeds of other aquatic plants. Most of their customers are sportsmen who want to lure waterfowl to their ponds, but gardener cooks with access to ponds and streams are also discovering that growing your own wild rice is a simple business. Wildlife Nurseries, P.O. Box 2724, Oshkosh, Wisconson, 54901, sells wild-rice seed and sprouted shoots. The seed is available both in fall (fresh) and spring (cold storage).

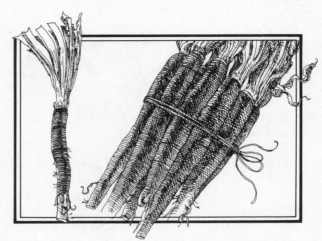

SCORZONERA

(*Scorzonera hispanica*)

Scorzonera is one of about 150 species of perennial plants with milky sap native to the Mediterranean countries and central Asia. The scorzonera of the garden, also known as black salsify, viper's grass, and black oyster plant, is grown from seed and treated as an annual. The roots are prepared like salsify but never peeled before cooking, while the long, narrow, deeply veined leaves can be enjoyed in salads.

The black-skinned roots are sweet and very good, with a flavor not unlike oysters in cream. There are several stories attached to the name *scorzonera*. One has it that the word is a misspelling of the Italian word *scorzanera* which means "black bark," but another says it is a corruption of the Catalan word *escorso*, which means "viper" and is a reference to the supposed power of scorzonera against snakebite.

Scorzonera is much superior in taste to salsify, which generally gets all the attention, probably because of its more appealing appearance. Scorzonera is never seen in American markets.

Scorzonera was a wild thing known only to plant gatherers until it began to be cultivated in Spanish gardens in the last quarter of the sixteenth century. In a short time it was growing in French, English, and Belgian gardens. It is likely that the plant was first grown as a medicinal herb for counteracting the effects of snakebite. Rhind tells the tale of how scorzonera was supposed to have gained its reputation as a snakebite palliative:

> A Moor . . . who had learnt in Africa that this plant possessed so valuable a property, availed himself of the knowledge in effecting many different cures with the juices of the leaves and roots upon peasants who had, while mowing, been bitten by these venomous reptiles; but he carefully concealed the plant, that he might

retain to himself all the honor and the profit attendant on the discovery. He was, however, clandestinely followed to the mountains where he was observed to collect this plant.... The knowledge was quickly disseminated.

By the late seventeenth century, scorzonera was a highly regarded culinary vegetable of considerable importance. Louis XIV, that great trencherman, had scorzonera in the royal kitchen gardens as a stomachic to ease the bouts of indigestion the royal interior was subject to after some marathon dinners.

Scorzonera lost its place as a leading vegetable in the nineteenth century, a casualty of Victorian fastidiousness. Scorzonera was regarded as a dirty object because of its black skin, which led to the lamentable habit of peeling the roots. The unique flavor and the vitamins were both discarded with the skins, and the fine root lapsed into obscurity. Only in the past few decades has Europe rediscovered scorzonera. In North America it remains an exotic. It is a far more rewarding crop for the gourmet gardener than salsify; scorzonera has the richer flavor and the larger, straighter roots.

Interplanted with carrots, scorzonera has the reputation of repelling carrot flies (to say nothing of snakes!). It is also, along with the Jerusalem artichoke, a useful vegetable for diabetics, for both roots contain insulin, though I can find no information on how cooking temperatures affect this substance.

There are several cultivars of scorzonera around, and some are bitter unless they are scrubbed and soaked in cold water for an hour before cooking. The soak water is discarded and fresh water put into the cooking pot. André Simon mentions the French scorzonera called *Picridie*, which is grown for its successive-cropping salad leaves rather than for the root, which in this cultivar is quite coarse. Sturtevant lists five species of scorzonera: *S. crocifolia*, a favorite in Greece for salad greens and for cooking like spinach; *S. deliciosa*, extensively cultivated in Sicily "on account of its sweet roots of very grateful flavor"; *S. Hispanica*, the type most generally available to gardeners; *S. parviflora*, which grew on the plains of western Asia and was used for its green leaves by the Kirghiz tribespeople; and *S. tuberosa*, grown in Turkestan. Vilmorin-Andrieux described both *S. hispanica* and the *Picridie* mentioned by Simon sixty years later.

Scorzonera seed is sown in midspring so that it will be ready to harvest in the cool autumn weather. It takes about four months to mature. Seed should be sown in light, rich sandy loam that has been deeply worked, even double-dug, to allow the roots to grow straight down. It is not too much to prepare a bed eighteen inches deep. Good rotted compost conditions the light soil and lets the roots extend easily. Clay soils force the roots to grow crookedly. Like most root crops, scorzonera needs a dependable supply of water for rapid and steady growth.

At harvest time, take great care in digging up the big roots. They are fairly brittle and, if broken or gouged, will leak copiously, so that much of the flavor will be lost. *Do not peel the roots*. Scrub them gently and soak for an hour before cooking. Add a little lemon juice or vinegar to the water to prevent discoloration.

Scorzonera is steamed or boiled until it is tender, about forty-five minutes. Then the roots are drained, and when they are cool enough to handle, the skins are rubbed off, in the same way that the skins of beets are removed. Recipes are not easy to find in our cookbooks, but European collections have many for scorzonera and salsify, and they are interchangeable. A favorite way of preparing them abroad is to cut the cooked roots into three-inch sections, dip them in batter, and fry them until they are crispy and brown; they are served with a dash of lemon juice. Scorzonera can also be prepared *gratiné*, in a vinaigrette sauce as a cold salad, browned in sizzling butter, and a dozen other ways, none of them to be missed.

Scorzonera seed is getting easier to find in our catalogs. It is offered by Redwood City, Le Jardin du Gourmet, Johnny's Selected Seeds (Gigantia), and William Dam (Pilotis, listed under salsify!), and no less than three cultivars are featured in the Urban Farmer. These are Pronora and Triplex, both from Holland, and the French strain of Giant Black of Russia. All three are available as an individually packaged scorzonera sampler.

SEA KALE

(Crambe maritima)

An exceptionally choice and luxurious dish is steamed, blanched sea kale served with melted butter or hollandaise sauce that lets the vegetable's exquisite flavor of hazelnuts touched with a faint bitterness melt on the palate. For centuries the blanched and tender young shoots and stalks of sea kale were cut in earliest spring by the natives of coastal England, Scotland, and Ireland, where the succulent vegetable originated. The thick, crinkly blue-green leaves that edge the stalks are trimmed off to make a fine salad dressed with oil and vinegar and chopped chives or a little fresh tarragon. The nutty flavor is present in the leaf as well as the stalk.

Sometimes sea kale stalks are tied in a bundle and boiled briefly until tender, then removed to a casserole, covered with Mornay sauce, and baked until hot and bubbling. No matter how it is prepared, the flavor and fine meaty texture are not easily forgotten.

The plant is a hardy perennial found along the seacoasts of the Atlantic, the North Sea, and the Mediterranean. Sturtevant says that the Romans knew it, gathered it in armfuls, and packed it into barrels for long voyages for its therapeutic virtues in preventing scurvy.

Sea kale remained only a regional delicacy well into the eighteenth century, but it was noted for sale in bundles of stalks at Chichester Market in 1753. The seed, Sturtevant tells us, "sold at a high price as a rarity," and by the end of the century it was grown as a "choice esculent" in many English gardens; it is still esteemed as a special treat. In nearly every issue of the popular Victorian gardening periodical *The Floral World and Garden Guide* there is an article on forcing sea kale. It was very much desired as a special dish for Christmas dinner, and again and again we find gardeners' directions for achieving a fine harvest of sea kale in December, no mean gardening feat. Wrote a correspondent in 1867, "This delicious vegetable is very tempting to the epicure, as displayed in the windows of the greengrocers' shops, in the clean punnets wrapped in fine paper, at this dreary season of the year...a dish of forced sea-kale for the family dinner on Christmas-Day." He then described several exceedingly complicated arrangements of pits, boxes, hotbeds, and the like for pushing along an out-of-season sea kale feast.

M'Mahon lists sea kale as a plant found in American gardens in 1806, and we know that in 1809 John Lowell of Roxbury, Massachusetts, started growing it; five years later he offered seeds of sea kale to the public. Another early seedsman, Thorburn, described sea kale in an 1828 catalog as "very little known in the United States, though a most excellent garden vegetable and highly deserving of cultivation." And that opinionated man, William Cobbett, who wrote on both sides of the Atlantic on cabbages and kings and spared neither vegetable nor monarch his ill-tempered criticism, has this to say about sea kale:

This is a capital article. Inferior in point of quality to no vegetable but the *Asparagus*, superior to that in the merit of *earliness*; and, though of the easiest propagation and cultivation, I have never seen any of it in America.... This is, unquestionably (after the asparagus) the very best garden vegetable that grows.

There are about twenty species of *Crambe* stretching from the Canary Islands to western Asia in habitat, but only *maritima* seems to be eaten. *C. cordifolia* is sometimes seen in European gardens as a striking ornamental with exotically showy flowers, and *C. hispanica* is grown in Mediterranean countries as a commercial oilseed crop.

Sea kale is a perennial that will give good yields of stalks for up to ten years. Like asparagus, it takes several years to establish the bed.

The seeds germinate easily and should be sown an inch deep in rich, loamy nursery-bed soil in direct sunlight. When the young plants are up, they should be thinned to six inches apart in the row. The young plants are weeded and watered during the first season and allowed to develop good root systems. A side-dressing of rotted manure or manure tea helps them along; sea kale particularly enjoys a thick seaweed mulch. I have read occasionally the advice that inland growers should sprinkle a tablespoon of salt around each sea kale plant, but I opt for the seaweed.

The second year, in the spring, the sea kale plants are transplanted to their permanent quarters or thinned out in the nursery bed to permanent places. Only the strongest and lustiest plants are chosen, and they are set three feet apart from one another. They are allowed to build up strength throughout this second year, also, much as an asparagus bed is tended but not harvested throughout its second season. In autumn the roots should be protected from frost with a good mulch.

In the spring of the third year the gardener can permit himself to take a modest first crop, perhaps 10 percent of the sea kale. In the early spring he goes daily to the sea kale bed and scrutinizes the earth near the plants. Cracks in the soil mean that the tender sea kale shoots are about to emerge. Now the gardener rushes to the potting shed and rummages about to find the equivalent of a sea kale pot, a tall pot ten inches in height that excludes all light, for the purpose of blanching the new and tasty shoots. (In the nineteenth century "Pascall's seakale pots" were the standard; they had lids that lifted up and allowed the gardener to peep inside and see how the shoots were coming along.) A big flowerpot with the hole plugged up or taped over with electrician's tape will do, though it is not as convenient as the lidded pots. A gardener handy in the shop can make wooden light-safe boxes with hinged lids.

The pots or boxes are set over the emerging shoots to keep them in the dark. When the shoots are seven or eight inches long, they are cut off or snapped near the ground and brought into the kitchen.

When leaves begin to appear on the shoots, the harvest is over, and the gardener withdraws from the sea kale bed. The kale pots are put away until the next spring, and the bed is weeded and dressed as in previous years. A well-established bed will continue to produce delicious shoots for six or seven years more.

Sea kale can be grown from cuttings called *thongs*, but you have first to find someone with a sea kale bed, not an easy matter in North America. However, should you wish to pass on cuttings from your own established bed to gardener friends, take the straight side shoots that grow out from the central sea kale root or crown. Thongs are generally cut in the fall. The best are about six inches in length and up to half an inch in diameter. In Europe the thongs are tied in neat bundles and stored overwinter in sand in a root cellar until spring planting. There is no reason why cuttings cannot be taken in the spring and planted immediately in the new bed, as long as the gardener gets there with his trowel early enough—sea kale sends up its shoots before any other plant in the garden. A small harvest can be taken the second year from beds established from thongs.

In England one can buy good sea kale thongs from nurseries. In North America we are fortunate to find seed. J. L. Hudson and Thompson and Morgan carry an unnamed sea kale cultivar. Bountiful Gardens, which carries the organically grown seed of the English firm Chase, has Lily White sea kale. Urban Farmer has a strain from Holland.

There are other ways of growing sea kale that merit some attention. English gardener Brian Furner wrote a chapter titled "Less Common Vegetables" in Kenneth A. Beckett's *The Gardener's Bedside Book* and in it described his way of getting early sea kale shoots:

> My own way is to plant thongs 18in. apart and allow strong crowns to develop. This takes two seasons, and I remove any flowering stems as soon as I see them. I lift the plants in November, cut off sufficient thick thongs . . . for replanting elsewhere in the garden, and set the rest of the roots closely together in the greenhouse border, cover with 2in. of sedge peat and spread a sheet of thick black polythene over the bed. I inspect carefully for

blanched foliage which, if the winter is very cold, may not be ready for cutting until the first week of April. When cutting sea-kale, dig the knife an inch or two into the ground and cut off the piece of root to which the white foliage is attached.

Sea kale can be forced in the same fashion as witloof chicory, that is, by digging up several very strong crowns in autumn and letting them rest in sand in a root cellar for a few months or so. About six weeks before the treat is wanted for table, the crowns are set in a box of soil and covered with an inch or so of light sandy soil or peat moss, then heavily watered. If the root cellar is dark, no cover is needed. If there is a window, cover the box with a few inverted flowerpots or a black plastic bag that has a few slits in it for ventilation. The temperature for forcing should be around 50 degrees F. Harvest the shoots when they are five or six inches long.

SORREL

(*Rumex* cultivars)

Travelers to India know a piquant green that appears in salads, soups, and curries as "sour-sour." It is the Indian sorrel, one of a large group of perennial herbs commonly called dock. The wild sheep sorrel (*Rumex aceto-cella*) of North America is the sourgrass so familiar to country children. The several garden cultivars—French sorrel (*R. scutatus*), garden sorrel (*R. ace-tosa*), and spinach-rhubarb (*R. abyssinicus*)—all have culinary uses, and the tangy sourness is welcome in spring salads. Sorrel is also pureed and served with shad, a classic accompaniment to that equally seasonal delicacy. It flavors soups and stews, accompanies poached eggs and stuffs omelets, and has a role as the main ingredient in some very lively and tart sauces. Its greatest role is as the star in a cold and creamy *potage Germiny* garnished with chervil. It is hard for us to realize how joyfully those first green salads of spring were greeted by our ancestors, who got through the winter without fresh vegetables.

For centuries sorrel was used in Europe and the Near East as a "blood cleanser" and as an antiscorbutic. It reached its height of popularity in the sixteenth century, when gardeners vied to grow it for both culinary and medicinal purposes. Said Parkinson, "Sorrell is much used in sawces, both for the whole and the sick, cooling hot livers and stomackes. . . . It is also a pleasant relish for the whole in quickening up a dull stomack that is overloaden with every daies plenty of dishes. It is divers waies dressed by cookes, to please their Masters stomacks."

Sorrel was an important part of the diet of northern Scandinavians, where fresh greens were missing for most of the year, and it is still much used in Scandinavian kitchens. In Cornwall, a regional delicacy, still occasionally found, is the "sour-sauce pasty," a sorrel tart that uses the stalks of the plant as we use rhubarb stalks to make pies.

Yet sorrel is not a pure blessing. All the sorrels contain varying amounts of oxalic acid, which gives the plants their distinctive tart flavor. But some people are allergic to this acid. Additionally, it is known that oxalic acid can prevent the absorption of calcium into the bloodstream.

Vilmorin-Andrieux lists three sorrels: *acetosa*, *scutatus*, and *montanus*, each with several cultivars. The most widely grown cultivar then and now was Belleville (*R. acetosa*), at one time grown year-round under frames for the Paris market, where, one assumes, it was consumed in *potage Germiny* by the bucketful. Our seed catalogs generally carry sorrel as an herb or odd vegetable. Le Marché Seeds International has Lyons sorrel, Redwood City sells Belleville de Chambourcy, and Le Jardin du Gourmet has an unnamed sorrel. J. L. Hudson alone sells *R. scutatus*.

Sorrel grows best in a light, loamy soil with moderately acid pH levels. The soil should have plenty of composted manure worked in and the manure tea barrel nearby, for sorrel is a heavy feeder, and although it is a perennial, good gardeners will move the bed every three or four years and plant the old plot to a restorative green-manure cover crop. Full sun and light shade both suit sorrel.

Sow the seed in early spring and, after the plants are up, thin them to stand twelve inches apart in the row. The plant is a vigorous grower and appreciates side-dressing of rotted manure and composted seaweed in spring and midseason, plus a dipperful of manure tea every two weeks. To prevent the rampant spread of sorrel throughout your garden, cut back the seed stalks when they appear. The plants will send out vigorous roots and runners and fill up the bed.

Keep the outer leaves picked frequently, even if you are sick of *potage Germiny* and have to put them on the compost heap; this keeps the tender center rosettes producing. Leaves left unpicked for too long become tough and disagreeable.

Should your sorrel plants escape their bounds and threaten your garden and grounds with takeover, the revolt can be subdued by sprinkling a little lime on them.

CHAPTER 4

THE LITTLE HERB GARDEN

Basil/Chervil/Coriander/Day Lily
Ginger/The Mints/Oregano/Rosemary/Sage
Summer Savory/Tarragon/Thyme

Two of the great pleasures of life are wine and food properly seasoned with herbs, but not very many decades ago both were rather uncommon in American cooking. Our increasingly sophisticated interest in gardening has led to the little herb garden outside our kitchen doors or on the winter windowsill, and we have learned to appreciate the richer, more complex tones of dishes augmented by the spicy fresh leaves. Truly fine cooking is linked inextricably with the knowledge and use of the fragrant culinary herbs, and it is certain palettes of associated herbs that give national and regional cuisines their distinctive characters. Garlic, oregano, and sweet basil are linked to Italian cooking; fenugreek and coriander are familiar in Indian dishes; chile, chocolate, and cumin tell us we are in Mexico. The *bouquet garni* of French cooking is the familiar parsley, bay leaf, thyme, sweet marjoram, and rosemary.

Stubborn adherents to the "plain meat and potatoes" school of cooking, which ventures not beyond the salt and pepper shakers for additional flavor, can be convinced by the Famous Roast Chicken Test. Two fresh chickens are prepared for roasting the day before the test. The plain chicken is left alone except for a sprinkle of salt in the interior. The herb-treated chicken is sprinkled inside with salt and pepper, and then the cavity is stuffed with two cloves of crushed garlic, a small onion cut in half, three or four sprigs of flat-leaved Italian parsley, four or five leaves of fresh sage, and a few celery or lovage leaves. A teaspoon of lemon juice is blended with two tablespoons of olive oil, and the exterior of the chicken is coated with the glistening mixture. More sage and parsley sprigs are tucked under the wings and in the crease where the legs join the body. The chicken is covered and set to chill overnight in the refrigerator with its plain companion. The next day the chickens are brought out of the refrigerator and allowed to warm to room temperature as the oven heats, then both are roasted in separate pans in the same oven. At last portions of breast and thigh meat are set before the Doubting Thomas for comparison. The chicken cooked with herbs is a ravishing dish. The plain chicken is—well, plain chicken, good enough in its way, but hardly the stuff of memories.

Besides the usual culinary herbs, every cook needs a collection of special seasonings to suit his or her personal tastes or favored cuisines. Today's gourmet gardener is rarely restricted to one style of cooking, but knows how to prepare specialties from China, Southeast Asia, Italy, the Caribbean, South America, Scandinavia, and Mexico as well as regional dishes from all around this country. It is important to have the correct fresh herbs at hand to achieve the distinctive flavors of each cuisine. Here are a few herbs that can make the vital difference between a pallid imitation and the real thing when they are used fresh and dewy from the kitchen garden.

Salad lovers appreciate herb oils. These richly flavored oils can be used not only in salads, but in sauces, on pizzas, in spaghetti, on chops and fish headed for the broiler, and in marinades. Fresh herbs, such as oregano or bay leaves or one of the basils, are placed in a clean glass jar, then covered with olive oil or other cooking oil and tightly capped. The jars stand in the sun on a windowsill for two or three weeks or until the oil has picked up a good aroma of the herb. The oil is decanted then and stored in a dark, cool place. Italian cooks toss the herb leaves they remove from the steeping jar directly into the spaghetti sauce simmering on the stove. (A particularly felicitous use of bay leaf herb oil is to marinate black olives in it along with mashed garlic and grated orange peel for twenty-four hours—exceptionally good.)

Indispensable adjunct of successful kitchen capers, the *bouquet garni* is varied to suit the dish. The great triumvirate is parsley, thyme, and bay leaf, used in soups, stews, poached fish, and even salad dressings and sauces. The variations on the *bouquet garni* are limited only by the cook's imagination and his herb garden. In Provence, game dishes are given a certain piquancy by adding a strip of dried bitter orange peel to the *bouquet garni*. In North

America, sage, celery, marjoram, and chives or other onion leaves give life to dishes with pork, sausage, or beef. Tarragon is much used in parts of France in *bouquets garnis* destined for the chicken pot. Basil, oregano, and garlic enter the *bouquet garni* in Italy. Fennel and sage are often added to *bouquets garnis*, and dill is pleasant when the dish is poached fish.

To make a *bouquet garni* of fresh herbs is simplicity itself. The sprigs are gathered and bound together with white thread immediately before they are used. Herbs are strongest in flavor when gathered in the morning before the summer sun has dissipated their aromatic oils. Some herbs strengthen as they dry—oregano, for example—but most of them become weak and insipid.

The culinary herbs have many more uses than in *bouquets garnis*. Cheese, creams, and butters will absorb herb flavors if allowed to stand overnight in close proximity to the fresh-picked leaves. Herb teas are presently enjoying a great vogue, and they are quite simple to make. A scant handful of fresh herb leaves is placed in a warmed teapot, and boiling water is poured over them. Two or three minutes of steeping are enough. Combinations of herbs and strawberry leaves are often very fine and allow the gardener to make up a private blend. Dried-herb teas are less interesting. Iced tea, lemonade, and fruit juices chilled overnight in the refrigerator with a few leaves of the various mints (orange, ginger, and pineapple mint are good) or a little angelica syrup are outstanding in hot weather. Borage flowers and the newest leaves from the growing tips have a unique cool flavor, and the flowers and leaves of some of the scented geraniums in an icy glass on a silver tray have no equal. Tomato juice (and its potent cousin, the popular Bloody Mary) is an excellent medium for herb enhancement. Borage, salad burnet, chives, sweet basil, marjoram, lovage, and oregano all give a wonderful kick to tomato-based drinks.

Herb jellies are not to be missed. Crab apple jelly flavored with a sprig of thyme swished through the seething mass just before it jells is ineffable served with hot biscuits and sweet butter. Jellies to accompany game dishes and holiday turkey are made with lemon thyme, rosemary, mint, marjoram, sage, summer savory—whatever combinations you like. I particularly enjoy a port wine and sage jelly with duck.

Herb-flavored breads are great country favorites. Pumpkin bread flavored with mint, basil, coriander, sage, and chives is a holiday gift from a friend every December that always draws cries of delight from the uninitiated. Basil, chervil, dill, marjoram, mint, oregano, thyme, savory, sage—all are good in breads. One of the best introductions to herb breads appeared as a series of articles in *The Herb Quarterly* some years ago. It is now in book form as *The Little Bread Garden*, and is available from *The Herb*

Quarterly, Newfane, Vermont 05345, for $2.95 plus postage.

Every herb gardener will enjoy *The Herb Quarterly*, an unusual magazine featuring scores of ways to grow and use herbs. A comprehensive book on herb gardening that contains designs for all types of herbal plots contributed by the farflung members of the Herb Society of America, from Canada to the Deep South, is *Herb Garden Design* by Faith Swanson and Virginia Rady. Gertrude B. Foster and Rosemary Louden's *Success with Herbs* remains a very solid treatment of herb culture and use and has colored photographs of scores of herb seedlings. Many beginning herb gardeners have pulled up their young herbs along with the little weeds because they could not identify them. Maretta Marcin's *The Complete Book of Herbal Teas* covers the subject from cultivation to steeping.

The herb garden can include hundreds of plants, from angelica to yarrow, but the culinary herb plot may be as small as a dozen indispensable favorites, the gardener adding others for particular uses as he or she gains interest. The top twelve herbs in North America are the basils, chives, dill, marjoram, the mints, oregano, parsley, rosemary, sage, savory, tarragon, and thyme. Most of these are so familiar to gardeners that only a few need any discussion, particularly those that have several cultivars or a confused nomenclature.

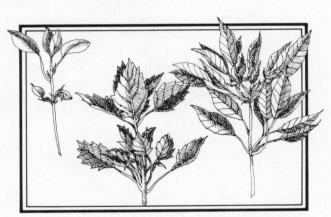

BASIL

(Oci-mum spp.)

In their native environment—tropical Africa and India—the basils are perennials, but in North America they are usually grown as tender annuals. Basil is sometimes still called "the king of herbs", an ancient name that goes back to the time of the Greeks, whose word *basilikon* means "kingly." There are about 150 species of the fragrant basils, and collecting those few that are available commercially is a delightful hobby for herb growers.

There are hundreds of legends, tales and myths associated with the basils, most of them linked to basil's double role as a symbol of both life and death, dating back to prehistoric times when the fragrant herb was used in religious ceremonies as a sacred plant. The Romans planted basil seed with much stamping and cursing, calling out to the gods to prevent it from sprouting, for the basils were thought to be contrary plants, which, if abused, would flourish. Some believed basil harmed the eyesight; others thought it deadened the pain of a scorpion bite. Up until the sixteenth century basil was much sought after by herbalists in England, but then its popularity waned, except as a seasoning in turtle soup. John Winthrop, Jr., brought "1 oz Bassill seeds at 3d" from England to Massachusetts Bay Colony, but whether it was grown in the sallet garden or the physick garden is not clear.

There are a number of different basils available, to the delight of the collector and the confusion of the beginning herb gardener. Almost all of them are soulmates to tomatoes in any form, whether eaten fresh in the sunny garden with olive oil and salt or in a tomato salad, soup, spaghetti sauce, or stuffed with seafood. All the basils are fairly delicate herbs that should be added to cooked sauces and dishes near the end, lest the volatile fragrance be carried away in the steam. Basil is never cut with a knife, but torn apart with the fingers for the best release of the scented oils.

Of the world's gastronomic treasures that lean on basil, *pesto*, a Genoese specialty, is probably the best known, although a Yugoslavian chicken soup, *tchorba*, is mentioned by Waverly Root in his magisterial *Food* as an outstanding basil-flavored dish. A very pleasant touch in some Italian restaurants is a small vase of fresh-picked basil leaves on the table, which sends out the spicy-bitter perfume to mingle with the aroma of the food.

Seven or eight basils are available today, though it is said that in the last century there were as many as sixty cultivars of sweet basil alone. Here are some of the most noteworthy.

Bush basil (*O. basilicum minimum*) is the finest of the basils for culinary use, though not the one most often planted in our herb gardens. It rarely grows taller than nine to twelve inches and has small, fine, aromatic leaves. Its small size and fine flavor make it an important herb for the kitchen windowsill. It is propagated by seed or cuttings and, like all the other basils, likes a fertile, well-drained soil with plenty of sunlight. If you plant this basil in a pot, be generous with its size.

Purple basil (*O. basilicum purpurascens*) has a very handsome coloring, but the fine purple color seems to be determined by a recessive gene, and if you keep your own seed, the plants in successive generations turn back to green-mottled or all-green leaves. A dwarf purple basil, once available to gardeners, has become rare and is much sought after.

One of the finest purple basils is Dark Opal, developed at the University of Connecticut around 1950. Dark Opal is a delicate, warmth-loving plant that cannot take chill or rough handling. It does best started inside in soil blocks six weeks or more before hardening off. Dark Opal plants should not be moved outside until the nights are fairly warm and all danger of frost has passed.

The taste of Dark Opal is drier and cooler than the other basils, and it is often grown for the vinegar bottle. It turns the vinegar a lovely raspberry-pink color and gives it a warm basil flavor. About one cupful of leaves is steeped in a quart of cider or pear vinegar in a sunny windowsill for up to a month, or until the color and flavor of the basil have passed into the vinegar. The leaves are removed from the finished vinegar, and it is poured into fancy bottles. Shops catering to cooks have begun to carry these handsome vinegar bottles of pressed glass in ornate shapes.

An Italian purple basil, Genovese Grand Violetto, is carried by Epicure Seeds, and it has a very fine color. Other purple basils are easy to find in the catalogs.

Holy basil (*Ocimum sanctum*) is a hairy, very pungent basil with a heavy, oily, spicy scent. The holy basil generally available here is the sacred herb of Hindu India. Another strain from Thailand, where it is known as By-Kra-pow, according to herb authorities Gertrude Foster and Rosemary Louden, has a musky odor. This variety is sometimes found in dried form in oriental grocery stores. Holy basil is used in sachets and potpourris, but it is also used in cooking in India and the Far East, where its rather strong flavor is balanced with that of chile peppers, fish paste, garlic, soy sauce, and pungent mushrooms.

Sweet basil (*Ocimum basilicum*) is bigger, coarser, and stronger in flavor than *minimum* and is the most common basil in our gardens. The plants grow up to two feet tall and are an important herb crop in California. Sweet basil is often interplanted with the tomatoes it so beautifully enhances.

Several of the sweet basil cultivars are of interest. The Lettuce Leaf Basil (*O. basilicum crispum*) is a big plant with leaves up to four inches long and a crinkled texture. It has a good flavor and is much used for pesto. An excellent way of keeping the flavor of fresh basil in the kitchen during the winter is to blend two cups of torn basil leaves fresh from the garden with a cup of water, then pour the green soup into an ice-cube tray and freeze until solid. The green basil cubes are then tipped into a plastic bag, sealed, labeled, and stored in the freezer until wanted. *Crispum* is a good basil for this treatment. Lettuce Leaf Basil is usually grown from seed. The leaves will waterspot if sprayed with cold water, and the appearance of the plant can be ruined with careless hosework. The seed is available from J. L. Hudson and a few others.

Lemon Basil (*O. basilicum citriodorum*) has a smooth, lemony scent that is very agreeable. This tender plant was introduced in 1940 from Thailand by the USDA, though it was known and described as early as Gerard's *Herbal* in 1597. The seed is always started outside after the soil is warm, for transplants tend to bolt or suffer a relapse from transplant shock. Lemon Basil is a favored flavoring for pea soup.

Licorice Basil and Cinnamon Basil are two more aromatic cultivars of sweet basil. They as well as Lemon Basil and Holy Basil, can be bought in a collection from Park Seeds.

Piccolo is a tiny Neapolitan basil much used in the cuisine of that city, and it is one of the best basils for pot culture. Epicure Seeds carries it.

Bush basil, Lettuce Leaf, and sweet basil can be started indoors six weeks before the last spring frosts are over. Basil seed started outside should be sown in warm, well-drained soil where plenty of sunlight falls. Basil also profits from a sheltered environment, and is often planted against a wall or rock ledge. Most of the basils germinate readily, but heavy rains can float the seed to ground surface, where it collects in a pile, dries out, and dies.

The passage from seed to maturity is swift—basil plants are ready to harvest in about seven weeks. As the plants grow, pinch back the growing tips to discourage flowering and to urge the plant on to greater leaf production, but once the flowering process has begun, it is not worth the effort to pinch it back, for the plant exhausts itself in an effort to make flowers.

Dried basil is so inferior to the fresh that it isn't worth the trouble of doing. Instead, cultivate two or three pots of basil for winter use and freeze up some herb cubes.

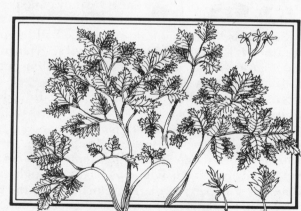

CHERVIL

(*Anthruscus cerefolium*)

Chervil is one of the oldest seasoning plants from northern Europe, a mildly piquant, pleasantly aromatic herb with a reputation for "chearing the spirits," as John Evelyn said.

Chervil has a distinguished place in French cuisine, and it is traditionally used in egg and fish dishes and many sauces. It is also good in green salads and in stews, added just before serving lest the delicate, aromatic oils all vaporize in the steam of long cooking. In ancient days chervil was popular as a dish of boiled greens seasoned with oil and vinegar. Gerard commends this recipe and bolsters it with the comment that boiled chervil "is very good for old people that are dull and without courage: it rejoyceth and comforteth the heart, and increaseth their lust and strength."*

In fact, chervil can be used in any way parsley is used, but the flavor is more subtle, with a faint aniselike taste. It is very nice in cold potato or cucumber salad and an elegant finish to cold tomato soup. Chervil is used sometimes as a substitute for French tarragon.

Unfortunately, chervil does not hold its volatile oil when dried. A better way of preserving the delicate flavor is by making herb ice cubes. Blend a cup of chervil leaves with one and one-half cups water in the blender, freeze in an ice-cube tray, then turn the ice cubes into a plastic bag. Twist the bag closed, label it, and store it in the freezer. Remove one of the herb cubes anytime you want fresh chervil flavor in your cooking.

If you are fond of *omelets fines herbes*, strip the leaves from chervil and sweet marjoram and add some chives. Freeze them mixed together in an airtight container. When you are making the omelet, chop the frozen leaves fine and use them as you would use the freshly gathered herbs.

Chervil does not transplant well, so it is sensible to sow seed where you want the herb. If you are given chervil seedlings by some well-meaning friend, they are apt to flower before they put out any good amount of leaves, and after all, it is the leaves we want.

Chervil is an annual, and it has the bad habit of bolting to seed in hot weather. It is traditional to sow chervil seed late in the summer so the plants can mature in the cooler days of approaching autumn. Chervil does best in moist, rich soil in partial shade.

The young seedlings should be thinned to twelve inches apart, and in France it is customary to hold off on this task until the little plants have two sets of true leaves. The thinnings are then added to an omelet for the taste of the first fresh chervil of the year. As chervil matures, the leaves change color to a beautiful shade of rose pink that looks very well in the salad bowl.

Chervil does well in windowsill pots throughout the winter and, in milder climates, can be grown under cloches or in the greenhouse.

Chervil butter is easy to make and adds wonderfully to the deliciousness of a fresh loaf of French bread. Chop several tablespoons of chervil leaves

---

*Quoted in Leighton, p. 272.

fine, then work them into half a pound of butter. Cover the dish and refrigerate for an hour or so before spreading it on the bread.

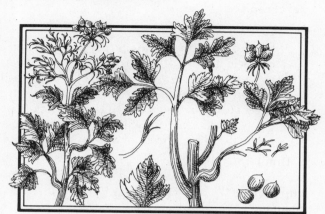

CORIANDER

(*Coriandrum sativum*)

This herb is also called cilantro. An annual plant, it is of easy culture in most garden soils, and considering its importance in Chinese cuisine as well as the food of Mexico, India, and the Caribbean, there is little reason why the gardener cook cannot have it fresh to hand. It is almost never found in the produce markets because it wilts quickly and cannot suffer much handling. It is familiar to curry aficionados, often accompanying dishes of great heat as a cooling complement. Both seeds and leaves are used in cookery.

The scent of coriander is reminiscent of orange or lemon peel and cumin to some, but the ancient Greeks thought it smelled of bedbugs. It is one of the oldest spices known, and seeds of coriander have been found at Bronze Age archeological sites. The Egyptians used it in wine, and in old Hindu religious ceremonies it was a magical herb with great powers. Coriander was a Roman favorite, too, and was put into many of their dishes, including a *bouquet garni* that included garlic, coriander, rue, mint, savory, onion, thyme, pennyroyal, and wild celery. Coriander fell somewhat out of favor during the medieval period, but was still used in many specialties. Elizabeth David, in her *Spices, Salt and Aromatics in the English Kitchen*, noted that at the White Hart Inn in Lewes, in the eighteenth century, one William Verral was known for his special way of simmering ham in milk with a bit of coriander.

Coriander came to the New World with the Spaniards and made a great success with Indians in South America and Mexico, where it became a staple spice. The Zuni Indians of the Southwest, says Waverly Root, still grow it to add the leaves to salads and the seed to chile and meat dishes.

The seeds have quite a different taste from the leaves. Says Root in a paragraph of praise,

> [I]t is at the same time sharply pungent and lightly sugary. For so egoistic a spice it is surprisingly versatile; it goes with almost everything, no doubt because of its contradictory nature, which permits it to be assertive and arrogant with game, pork or in sausage; subtly caressing with lamb, chicken or fish; unobtrusive in curry powders, from which it is almost never omitted; exotic in blood pudding, cheese or omelets; peppery with rice, mashed potatoes, Chinese noodles or Oriental soup; fiery in Ethiopian *berbere* sauce; and pungent in bread, cakes, puddings or confectionery.

Certainly in Cantonese cooking it is commonly used to flavor fish. Martha Dahlen and Karen Phillipps wrote *A Popular Guide to Chinese Vegetables* as a guide to the open-air markets of Hong Kong, but the first American edition (New York: Crown Publishers, 1983) includes marvelous and authentic recipes, including Fish and Coriander Soup and Thick Minced Beef and Coriander Soup, both with plenty of freshly shredded gingerroot and finely chopped fresh coriander leaves.

Growing coriander as an annual is not difficult, and the plant can be used from the first thinning to the frosts of autumn with successive plantings. It cannot take transplant trauma, so it is sown thickly *in situ* in early spring, then thinned out. Coriander likes full sun and needs it to develop a thick and bushy form. Some gardeners pinch the main growing tips to force the plant toward fullness.

Only a few years ago it was impossible to find coriander seed in North American seed catalogs; evidence of its growing popularity is clear when we see it offered now as a commonplace in the herb sections of many. Coriander is offered by Plants of the Southwest, J. L. Hudson, Redwood City, Johnny's Selected Seed, and many others.

DAY LILY

(Hemerocallis fulva)

The day lilies are enjoying an unprecedented popularity in North America, and not just the dull, muddy orange lily that grows along byways and in the margins of fields, a runaway from cultivation, but in hundreds of luscious colors: bronze, crimson, blue-red, apricot, tangerine, pink, cerise, fawn, gold, cream—subtle blends and tints merging and blending in the big flowers, many of them the new hybrid doubles. Day lilies are hardy perennials that grace any garden or border, and growers who dabble in oriental cooking know that they have many edible and delicious parts.

In China and other Asian countries the young stems of day lilies are steamed and served in the same fashion as asparagus are here. Flower buds as well as open flowers are added freshly picked to stir-fried dishes, or dipped in a batter and deep-fried. The flowers can also be added to salads, raw. They are generally torn apart rather than put in whole. The flavor is mild and agreeable. In oriental grocery stores one sometimes finds dried "golden needles" to be added to stir fries and soups. These are dried day lily buds.

The tubers are also edible and can be baked, steamed, roasted, or stir-fried. They have a delicious, sweet taste with a slightly smoky afterflavor. As if all this were not enough, all the parts of the day lily are a good source of protein.

Different cultivars are usually planted for the fine show of multiple colors and to ensure that something is always in blossom. *H. fulva*, the old familiar orange type, is the best day lily for the kitchen, with its good blossoms, tender stems, and delicious root, but it is a self-sterile triploid and rarely sets seed. It is propagated by division. There are a number of *fulva* cultivars around, some of them with distinct rose-colored tones blushing over the orange. Cypriana has big, brownish-orange blossoms; Kwason has double flowers. Maculata has large flowers banded with purple inside. Rosea has rose-tinted petals, and Virginica is a double orange flower blushed with rich rose.

The Lemon Day Lily (*H. lilioasphodelus*) also has very good flowers and stems for kitchen use, but the rhizomes are smaller than *H. fulva*. The fragrance of the flowers, which bloom in late spring, is sweet and reminiscent of orange blossoms. A Japanese dwarf species, *H. minor*, is a small lily with a yellow flower much enjoyed in Asian cooking, as is the Chinese Lily *H. aurantiaca*, its big orange flowers flushed with purple so that they seem a brownish color.

Day lilies are easy to grow. They manage in deep shade, dappled partial shade, or full sun, but prefer well-drained, medium-quality soil that is not too rich. They are an excellent plant for steep slopes and banks where erosion is a problem, and the underground rhizomes spread vigorously until the flowers form great, beautiful clumps. These clumps should be divided in spring or fall. Use the delicious tubers in the kitchen when you have all the bloom of day lilies you desire in the garden.

Day lily stock is available from many nurseries and horticultural suppliers.

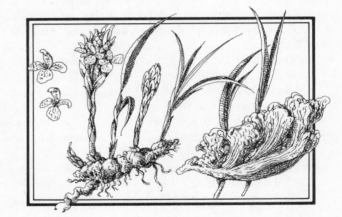

GINGER

(*Zingiber officinalis*)

Ginger is a tropical, rhizomatous herb that grows in clumps. Stem ginger and fresh gingerroot are indispensable in Asian cooking from China through the Pacific Islands to India. Many of the fine dishes of Polynesia, Micronesia, the Malay Archipelago, Indonesia, and the Philippines as well as China depend upon lime juice and fresh ginger for their exceptional flavor. It is fairly easy today to buy sound gingerroot in the supermarket produce section, but much of the time the root is old, stringy, tough, and flavorless. Fresh gingerroot is juicy, bright ocher yellow, and so crisp you can snap it apart. Stem ginger is the pale pink, juicy, and delicately flavored stems that rise from the rhizomes when they are planted, and it can be raised in the kitchen greenhouse or in a pot on the windowsill.

In Chinese cooking, a subtle but distinctive change in the taste of raw foodstuffs occurs at the moment they go into the hot cooking oil, for the oil is usually seasoned with a few slices of gingerroot before the shrimp or chicken shreds or vegetables are put in, much as Italian cooks season the olive oil in the pan with a smashed clove of garlic.

The delicate, crunchy stem ginger can be used chopped in soups, added to delicate fowl and fish dishes, or pickled in a light vinegar brine for an unusual, crisp relish. The stems can also be candied and used in confections and for cake decoration.

To grow gingerroot and stems, select sound, firm rhizomes that show sprouting points on the knobs. Several specialist seed houses offering oriental plant material have gingerroot, and occasionally so do nurseries. If all else fails, go to the supermarket and look over the rhizomes in early spring. The mail-order house Mellinger's carries good gingerroot.

A large pot, twelve to fourteen inches in diameter, is adequate for growing ginger stems. Light soil mixes containing one part good garden soil, one part compost, and one part sand make a nice medium for ginger. Lay the rhizomes on their sides with the sprouting knobs uppermost and cover with half an inch of soil. Water the pot well and place it in a sunny window. Keep the soil moist and warm.

After the sprouts appear, you may fertilize the ginger with a manure tea or your favorite plant-food mixture once in a while. The rhizomes will continue to produce sprouts for several months before the foliage dies back and the plant goes dormant. If you haven't cut too greedily at the tender stems, the rhizomes will have doubled in number. If you grow just for the rhizomes, let the stems grow freely without cutting them and, after the leaves die back, dig up the rhizomes. Save some of the best-looking ones for the next year's crop. Store them, like potatoes, in a cool, dark, dry place.

THE MINTS

(*Mentha* spp.)

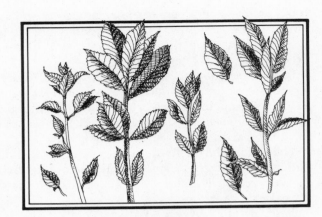

One often reads in gardening books that there are hundreds and hundreds of mints, but the sounder view is that there are about twenty-five species of these perennial plants, whose free and easy habit of hybridizing among themselves has led us to count more than six hundred "species." Most of the hybrids are sterile, but some are fertile, and a dozen or so are distinctive and much grown for their essential oils or use as culinary herbs.

Originating in temperate regions of Europe, the mints are generally hardy perennials that grow rapidly and densely. They are hungry feeders and can quickly exhaust the soil of their bed. The plants in the middle of the depleted bed will die out, while the vigorous newer growth in the suburbs will creep on to greener pastures. Mints die down in the cold weather and emerge again in spring in a burst of vigorous, minty green.

Rich, moist soil is what mints like best, and they are often grown along streambanks, where they generally do very well. Rust and slugs are mint afflictions, and rust can be particularly disagreeable if one is gathering sprigs for garnishing and iced tea.

The kitchen uses of mint are many. It is steeped as hot teas and added to juices; it garnishes cocktails, roast lamb, fruit salads and desserts; chopped fine, it is mixed into wheat salads of the Middle East; it is added to jellies and sauces, candies and liqueurs. The English favor mint in their cooking, and this writer can remember enjoying a minty cream soup in London a decade ago.

Mint can be grown in pots and containers. It can be used with good results as a ground cover in partially shady areas and is sometimes planted as a companion among the cole crops to keep preying insects at bay with its minty effusions.

The most commonly used culinary mints are spearmint, peppermint, apple mint, pineapple mint, red mint, orange mint, golden mint, and Corsican mint. Mint is propagated by cuttings, and every plant nursery offers a good choice of cultivars. Set the plants in sunny, moist, rich ground and stand back.

Spearmint (*Mentha spicata*) is familiar to most gardeners, identifiable by its erect stems, bright-green toothed leaves, and distinctive flavor. Spearmint was thought by the ancients to be the most useful of the mints, for it could ease headache and "stayeth the Hicket." It dried up watering eyes, took the pain of bee sting away when applied as a poultice, and prevented conception. Ann Leighton, in her *Early American Gardens*, cites an authority declaring spearmint to be "taken inwardly against Scolopenders, Bearewormes, Sea-scorpions, and serpents," afflictions that beset our ancestors more readily than they do us. Mints were also used to spark the intellectual to study, and as a preventative against the bites of mad dogs. It had some use in the medieval kitchen to flavor mackerel and other fish, to liven up puddings (some mints were so much used for puddings that they were called pudding grass), and as flavoring for "pease that are boyled for pottage."

In those ripe days of yore when cottage and castle dining rooms were fetid with yesterday's bones beneath the table and the careless hygiene of the diners themselves, mint was strewn about on the floors so that when it was trodden, it released a breath of clean, minty fragrance. Outdoor garden walkways were frequently planted with thyme, burnet, and the low-growing mints, especially Corsican mint.

Peppermint (*M. piperata*) is the other famous mint, the stuff of candy canes and peppermint schnapps. It has a snappier, stronger menthol taste than spearmint. There are many cultivars of peppermint and they are generally divided into two loose groups: "black peppermint," which has purple stems, and "white peppermint," which does not. Black peppermint yields greater amounts of the pungent menthol-flavored oil and is an important crop in the United States, which supplies the world with 75 percent of its oil of peppermint. There are some regional peppermints. Waverly Root mentions "Mitcham mint," which is grown in Mitcham, Surrey, England, and is thought to be the offspring of the original peppermint discovered in 1696 in Hertfordshire. France's peppermint comes mostly from Milly-la-Forêt, where it is grown as a cash crop.

Apple mint (*M. suaveolens*) is a woolly-leaved mint with vaguely apple-scented leaves. It is esteemed by some for making candied mint leaves with egg white and powdered sugar. The fuzzy leaves take the coating better than smooth-leaved types.

Gertrude Foster, in her *Success with Herbs*, notes an English cultivar, Bowles Mint, used there for mint jellies and sauces.

Pineapple mint (*M. suaveolens variegata*) is an exceptionally beautiful mint with mottled cream and green leaves. It is used in chilled cream-and-pineapple bombes and as a fruit-cup garnish. The young foliage has an intense pineapple scent.

Orange mint (*M.* x *piperata* var. *citrata*) has very dark green, heart-shaped leaves with purple stems and leaf edges. It is a sprawling plant that blooms with tiny pink flowers. The scent of citrus mixed with menthol makes a nice addition to iced fruits and drinks.

Red mint (*M.* x *gentilis*) has distinctively purple-red stems and dark-green, toothed leaves that have a spearmint-and-ginger scent. It is also grown commercially for its oil, and gardeners may find it in nurseries labeled Scotch mint, Emerald, or Gold mint. It is propagated from root divisions. One cultivar, Variegata, has golden lines along the midrib and main leaf veins and is extremely handsome in a scented bouquet.

Corsican mint (*M. requienii*) is a low, creeping plant with tiny round leaves. It is sometimes called the crème-de-menthe plant, for this is the cultivar used to flavor that liqueur. It makes a very nice ground cover, particularly between flagstones where passersby will inevitably crush a few leaves under foot, sending up the heady mint scent. Corsican mint is not very hardy and can rarely survive winters where the temperature drops below 5°F.

Rosemary, the mints, the sages and basils, the leaves of scented geraniums, woodruff, costmary, and many, many other herbs alone or in combination make a very pleasant and relaxing tub when added to hot bathwater. Tie the fresh sprigs with a bit of string and toss into the tub as it fills.

OREGANO

(*Origanum* spp.)

One of the most confusing tasks for gardeners who love to cook is sorting out the oregano from the marjoram; it is a devilishly tricky business, helped not at all by seed companies, who omit the Latin names.

Origanum is a group of about fifteen to twenty species of shrubby plants that originated in a region extending from the Mediterranean to central Asia, habitués of dry, rocky soils. Some of the family are tender annuals, others hardy perennials. One of the group, *O. majorana*, is better known as the culinary herb sweet marjoram, a tender annual that is delicate and spicy-sweet, and produces a fine oil.

Widely offered in the seed catalogs as "oregano" is *O. vulgare*, a highly variable species with many cultivars that have variegated leaves in yellow or golden or green. Gardeners who innocently grow this, expecting the pungent, spicy stuff of pizzas and fine Italian cooking, will be badly disappointed. *O. vulgare* is *not* the desirable culinary oregano, and seedsmen who say it is ought to be whipped with stinging nettles. Truth in advertising doesn't seem to apply to seed catalogs.

The lovely, spicy oregano of Mediterranean and Near East cuisines is *O. heracleoticum*, closely related and similar in appearance to *O. vulgare*, but with far more flavor and verve. *O. vulgare* has purple or white flower spikes, and the culinary oregano, *O. heracleoticum*, has spikes of white flowers. To tell the difference between the two, pinch the leaves—the rich, heady aroma of Neapolitan sauces will tell you that you have *O. heracleoticum*, but if you get only a pale, insipid ghost of flavor, you are probably growing *O. vulgare*.

O. heracleoticum is unreliable in seed form, for the plants are often cross-pollinated when they are in flower, and offspring are throwbacks to less desirable ancestors. Gardeners must look for this plant at herb nurseries. Dorothy Patent, in her brief article, "Found at Last—Real Oregano," in the

September 1983 issue of *Organic Gardening*, lists four nurseries that carry culinary oregano. These are:

Hilltop Herb Farm
P.O. Box 1734
Cleveland, Texas 77327

Sunnybrook Farms Nursery
9448 Mayfield Road
P.O. Box 6
Chesterland, Ohio 44026

Sandy Mush Herb Nursery
Route 2
Surrey Cove Road
Leicester, North Carolina
28748

Well-Sweep Herb Farm
317 Mount Bethel Road
Port Murray, New Jersey
07865

Nearby herb growers and nurseries may very well carry the pungent herb.

Fortunately, there is another plant that comes very close to *O. heracleoticum* in flavor and that can be grown from seed. It is generally offered in the catalogs as "Greek oregano." These are low-growing, small plants, and there are several types around, all strong and good in flavor. The Latin nomenclature is extremely vague, with one expert naming *O. dictamnus*, which grows wild in the mountains of Greece and Crete but is not very hardy. Another writes that Greek oregano is *O. vulgare viride*, with strong-flavored leaves and white flowers, again, not very hardy. Two catalogs which offer this call it simply Greek oregano or say it is "true oregano, collected wild in the mountains of Greece." *O. dictamnus* makes a nice little pot plant, and growing it indoors avoids trouble with low winter temperatures.

Seed of "Greek oregano" is available from Johnny's Selected Seeds and Otto Richter and Sons, Ltd. Another source of seed is in Greek specialty grocery stores, where imported flowering oregano tops (usually with some seed intact) are sold.

ROSEMARY

(*Rosmarinus officinalis*)

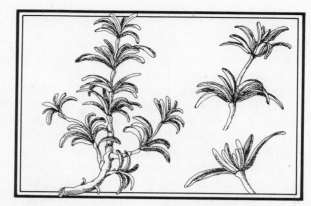

Several species of evergreen shrubs are native to the Mediterranean shores and are about as hardy as lavender. The pungent, resinous tops are distilled and used in perfumes and medicines, but the most familiar use is in culinary seasoning.

Rosemary is frequently left out of the herb section of gardening books, particularly books that deal with the beautiful but low knot gardens, because it is a woody shrub that can grow taller than a tall man and stouter than a stout man. The pungent, resinous evergreen needles are used to flavor hundreds of dishes, including pizza, jellies, biscuits and breads, stews and soups, casseroles, roast pork, spring lamb, and the first garden peas. It makes pleasant tisanes and teas and is a traditional aromatic in sachets and potpourris. Used as a rinse for dark hair, it gives gloss and fragrance.

One can never have too much rosemary. Unfortunately, gardeners who live in cold climates never have enough. Rosemary is a native plant of the Mediterranean coast, and its name is supposed to mean "dew of the ocean." Travelers report recognizing the clear scent of rosemary off the coast of Spain or Portugal while still at sea. Rosemary likes a mild climate, gravelly, sandy alkaline soil, fogs and mists and a stiff sea breeze. Potted rosemary grown on the windowsill often suffers from roots that are either too wet or too dry.

So ancient is rosemary, and so versatile an herb, that it has been a garden favorite literally for millennia. Many cultivars have been developed over the ages, from the trailing *R. officinalis prostratus*, to pink-flowered and blue-flowered types, to kinds with soft-gray foliage. In California a creeping rosemary is often used as a landscape plant on steep banks and to flow down stone retaining walls.

In mild climates rosemary will winter over, but in harsher winters the gardener must forego Mediterranean dreams and pot the rosemary.

Rosemary can be started from seed indoors in a flat. Germination is slow (two to three weeks), and growth is slow. The little plants should be potted in a sandy soil. Set them in the mild-climate garden well apart, for a robust plant can swell up to five feet in width.

Rosemary is often propagated by cuttings, and the best are taken in spring as the plant develops its new growth. Cuttings taken in the fall or winter, when the plant is in a dormant mode, will be slow to root. The cuttings are inserted into a sandy potting medium and covered with a clear plastic pot, which is adjusted to control condensation so that the interior is misty but moisture drops do not rain down on the cutting. The pots are set in good light but away from direct sunlight. It may take several months before the cuttings root. Treating the cutting with a plant hormone before setting it in the pot will encourage good root development.

Rosemary can also be layered outdoors where the climate is agreeable. Peg a low side branch to the ground in spring and heap soil on it. At the end of the summer cut the branch off the parent plant; it will have developed its own root system and can be transferred to a pot for an indoor life, or set in another location in the garden.

Overwatering is a constant danger with potted rosemary. Seaweed fertilizer is gratefully accepted by the plant.

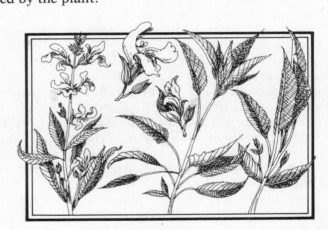

SAGE

(*Salvia officinalis*)

Life without sage is unthinkable. Only a few of this large group of shrubs and herbs are used in the kitchen, though dozens are familiar to ornamental growers for their handsome, variegated leaf colors. The prince of the kitchen is *Salvia officinalis*, a small, woody-stemmed shrublet with the familiar pebbly, gray-green leaves. Fresh sage is far superior to the dried stuff—

milder, sweeter, less dominating. It lacks the odd mustiness that dried sage sometimes has.

The ancient Druids supposedly fancied that sage was so powerful it could raise the dead, and the belief was perhaps at the root of the old adage "Why need a man die, if sage grow in his garden?"

Sage is one of the most ancient of cultivated herbs and was known to humankind from a very remote time. Cadmus, in Greek mythology, is supposed to have discovered that sage had healing properties (the herb was an important one in the medicinal garden of the past), and the Greeks made offerings to him on that account. The ancients apparently caught vipers by carrying about a branch of sage, which reputedly had the power to stupefy snakes. Toads were thought to live under sage plants, down among the roots, where their breath envenomed the entire plant. Anyone who happened to pluck and eat a leaf of a toad-poisoned sage was fated to die. The risk was great, since sage was used in the medieval period as a tooth cleaner, being briskly rubbed over the teeth.

S. officinalis, the most desirable culinary sage, has a number of cultivars. Tricolor has leaves of gray-green and white bordered with purple. Purpurea's leaves are a shade of red-violet. Albiflora bears charming white flowers in May or June.

Salvia clevelandii, sometimes called blue sage, is a tall, twisting shrub that grows in southern California, and it is a good substitute for *S. officinalis* in the kitchen, one of the very few sages that comes close to the spicy, rich scent we love.

Pineapple sage (*S. elegans*) has handsome red flowers in late summer and is a tall (four feet), leggy plant that is tender to frost. The pineapple aroma is very nice when a leaf is pinched a little before a sprig is added to fruit cups and drinks. The chopped leaves are good worked into cream cheese for a sandwich filling or cracker spread.

S. sclarea is clary sage, and it does not enjoy a good press today, though two centuries ago it was considered quite the thing in omelets. The plant has a very strong, almost unpleasantly crude scent. Still, it might be an acquired taste. Some people dip it in batter and deep-fry it to make clary fritters. Clary sage oil is used by perfumers as a mixer to smooth out the harsh odors of artificial scents.

There are other sages in other places. In France, the common sage is called *grande sauge*, and it is in every garden. More desirable is the *petite sauge de Provence*, with smaller, whiter leaves and a more intensely aromatic perfume. Catalogne sage has even smaller leaves and is used for cooking in southwestern France. None of these regional sages is available through our seed catalogs, though traveling gardeners might pick up some seed on the plants' home territory.

Sage, like many fragrant plants, is free of pests and diseases. It is a hardy, strong plant that makes an excellent background in the perennial border and especially sets off blue, purple, and magenta flowers and the golds and yellows. Common sage can make it through the winters in zone 4, but the fancy and variegated sages will die back even in harsher areas of zone 5.

Late-summer cuttings of sage can be potted and grown on the windowsill throughout the autumn and winter, just the time when it is most appreciated in holiday birds and homemade sausage. In the spring these pot plants can be turned out of their clay prisons and set in the garden bed.

Starting sage from seed is simple, though germination of the big seeds is somewhat slow—up to three weeks in a medium kept around 65 degrees f. Set the plants out in the garden after the frosts are over and after a hardening-off period of about ten days that includes increasing exposure to sunlight. Set the plants two feet apart to give them room to expand.

Sage is useful in scores of dishes besides turkey and sausages. The French pickle sage leaves, which make an unusual and good garnish or side relish. They also use sage in more imaginative ways than American cooks—to flavor marinades, threaded into meats that are to be roasted, plastered over small birds, and tied in place with string before they are cooked. Thrushes are traditionally wrapped in sage leaves. Green beans, peas, and broad beans often have a tender sage leaf thrown into the pot with them while they are steaming. Sage vinegar is made like other herb vinegars and used in salads and marinades.

SUMMER SAVORY

(Satureja hortensis)

Summer savory, or sweet savory, is a hardy annual with a rich, aromatic flavor. It has narrow, dark-green leaves with pale-pink flowers in the leaf axils. It is commonly sown from seed directly in the garden as soon as the ground can be worked. Many gardeners get the habit of letting a few plants go to seed at the end of each season, and because summer savory is such a willing grower, they are always in good supply. Thin seedlings to twelve inches apart.

Summer savory is an agreeable plant for first-time gardeners to try. The seedlings transplant easily. Start seed indoors, if you like, in a potting medium. The seed will germinate in about a week. Set the young plants out in the garden when they are about six inches high. Space set-out plants a foot apart.

Summer savory can become so top-heavy that the leafy tips of branches drag on the soil. It helps to supply a support, something as simple as a stake at the end of each row and a stout string to hold up drooping branches.

Summer savory reaches its finest hour in the flavoring of beans, especially broad beans, but don't hesitate to add a few leaves to the simmering pot of green beans or to crumble a teaspoonful of dried summer savory into baking beans. In Germany summer savory is called *Bohnenkraut*, or "the bean herb." It is equally fine in a cream sauce for broccoli, in cream of cauliflower soup, in a zucchini casserole, in the glazing for tender carrots. It is joyfully received in an oil-and-vinegar salad dressing. Try it, too, in scrambled eggs, in sausage and stuffings, and in stews and casseroles.

The traditional pairing of summer savory with beans, peas, and other "windie pulses" occurred in ancient days because the herb was thought to "marvelously prevail against the winde." A poultice of summer savory leaves was thought to take the pain out of bee stings.

Summer savory is usually harvested twice a season, in June and September, for drying. Cut the tops of the plants in the morning before the sun has drawn off the volatile oils. If the leaves have soil on them, rinse them well and shake dry. Spread the sprigs out on a drying screen, which can be as simple as a yard of nylon netting tacked onto a simple frame. Hang the drying screen in a shady but breezy place. Turn the sprigs daily until they feel quite dry. This dryness is usually deceptive. There is still moisture in the leaves, and when they are enclosed in a jar, they will mold. It is essential to finish off air-dried plant material by putting the plants in an oven that has been warmed to about 100 degrees F for ten or fifteen minutes, or until the leaves are dry enough to crumble in the hand. Do not bump the oven temperature up higher in an effort to get it over with quickly; the higher temperatures will drive off the aromatic oils.

Tarragon

(*Artemesia dracunculus*)

The artemesias are a far-flung tribe of about two hundred species of herbs and shrubs suited to poor, dry soil in the Northern Hemisphere. Some are fine ornamentals; others are grown for their medicinal or aromatic character. The French are ardent champions of tarragon, which they use in *bouquets garnis* along with chervil and chives in several classic sauces—hollandaise, Béarnaise, béchamel—and in salads, particularly with the heavier Romaine lettuces and slightly bitter endives. Tarragon also goes into French mustards and vinegar. Steamed asparagus and artichokes are often served with tarragon butter. So freely do the French use tarragon that *A. dracunculus* is often called French tarragon.

Gardeners looking for the seed of tarragon in their catalogs must beware of one of the seedsman's ploys; sometimes what is offered is not *A. dracunculus* but the sly false tarragon, *A. dracunuloides*, a.k.a. "Russian tarragon." This six-foot-tall impostor is virtually tasteless. Even if you do find the seed of *A. dracunculus*, "the true," do not rejoice until you actually see plants growing. The seed of French tarragon is usually infertile, and the plant is almost always propagated by division. This is another herb that should be bought at the herb nursery, not through the seed catalog.

Once you get home with your French tarragon plants, set them in medium-textured, well-drained soil. They can stand varying light intensities, from light shade to full sun. If you are getting your plants from a friend's divisions, it should be in early spring, and you can set the plants out twelve to twenty-four inches apart. If you get root cuttings, start them inside, then plant out in the bed. Keep the plants weeded, give them a good soaking every week or ten days during drought conditions and an occasional shot of manure tea, and they will thrive.

Tarragon is hardy to zone 4, but gardeners in harsher climates can keep it going by cutting back the plants in late fall and mulching them heavily. Tarragon also makes a fairly attractive pot plant, with its narrow, twisted leaves and curving stems.

Tarragon does not dry well. The fragrant oil disappears. If you cook a good deal with this herb, it is sensible to keep a pot of it growing on the windowsill. Tarragon cubes can be made by pulverizing fresh leaves in the blender with water to cover, then freezing them in an ice-cube tray. Package the frozen cubes and use them whenever needed throughout the winter for the delectable, almost-fresh flavor.

Harvest tarragon leaves when the plant is about a foot high. The most resinous and tender leaves are those at the tips of the branches.

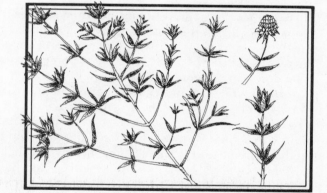

THYME

**(*Thymus*
spp.)**

The thymes are aromatic, small, and ancient perennial herbs and shrubs that extend in habitat from Europe to Asia. The Greeks were known to anoint themselves with thyme and oil, and Waverly Root tells us of one Dionysius of Syracuse, who gave an extraordinary party that featured wild thyme strewn throughout the palace for its heady, aphrodisiacal effects on the guests.

The wild thyme of the Mediterranean cliffs is an herb whose uses antedate history; it was known to the ancient Sumerians as early as 3500 B.C. That food of the gods, the honey of Mount Hymettus, was wild-thyme honey. The Egyptians used thyme as one of the fragrant herbs in their embalming unguent. Thyme was included in early lists of medicinal herb mixtures and was a seasoning for many dishes from salads to stews.

Over the centuries thyme became deeply rooted in European folklore and was often associated with the dead. It was also considered useful for dispelling troublesome demons or nightmares. Margaret Baker's *The Folklore of Plants* notes that the Welsh still plant thyme on graves, and "The Order of Oddfellows carry sprigs at funerals which are thrown into the grave of a dead member." In England the scent of thyme is sometimes seen as a symbol of murder. There is a path near Dronfield in Derbyshire where a young girl was murdered by her sweetheart long ago, and where, according to local inhabitants, the scent of thyme still persists.

Wild-thyme honey is one of the delectable prizes of the table; more ordinary honeys can be flavored with thyme by heating the honey with fresh thyme leaves in it and then straining it back into the jar. Thyme jelly is a good substitute.

The thymes of the table are not the wild thymes of legend, but more intensely fragrant, sweeter, and highly variable in their different perfumes. There are three hundred to four hundred species of thymes, many of them grown in rock gardens and along walkways for the pleasure of strollers, who stir the fragrant plants with their garments or tread them underfoot, releasing scent as evocative and fine as a few poignant piano notes heard in childhood and remembered a lifetime later.

Hortus Third, the authoritative botanical dictionary of plants, says, dryly, "Most thymes grown in America appear to be of confused identity and often erroneously named." *Thymus vulgaris*, or the common garden thyme, is the herb with so many and such varied cultivars that we grow in our gardens. English Thyme and French Thyme are two of the most popular *T. vulgaris* cultivars. English Thyme is broad-leaved and has a reddish tinge on the underside of the leaves. It is much used in the kitchen and is generally propagated from cuttings or division. The early horticultural writers called it "hard Time." French Thyme, also sometimes called Narrowleaf or Winter Thyme, has wiry stems and narrow leaves of the grayish-green color common to desert plants. Two other *T. vulgaris* cultivars are the so-called silver-leaved and gold-leafed thymes—*Argenteus* and *Aureus*, as they are named.

Thymus citriodorus is the Lemon Thyme of clear citrus flavor. It also comes with leaves dappled in variegated colors. *T. caespititius* is native to the Azores and Canary Islands and gives off the scent of tangerine peel. It is one of the many creeping thymes that make clumps and hummocks and mounds of fragrant little leaves with pink and lavender flowers. From Corsica and Sardinia comes the Caraway Thyme, *T. herba-barona*, a fine ground cover with deep-green leaves and little purple flowers. It is a fine culinary herb that, when crushed between the fingers, gives off the fragrance of caraway seed. The Creeping Thyme or Mother-of-Thyme that grows wild in

Greece and other Mediterranean countries is *T. serpyllum*, and *Hortus* says it is rarely grown in this country; instead, plants offered as *T. serpyllum* usually turn out to be any one of half a dozen other species. A number of gardening books describe many cultivars of *T. serpyllum* with such names as Pink Chintz and Splendens. *Caveat emptor!* The only way to be sure is to trot off to Greece and get a division of the real thing, and, of course, U.S. Customs frowns on the casual importation of live plant material.

T. vulgaris can be grown from seed. Germination is slow—up to a month—and the flat should be cool, around 55 degrees F. The plants should be set out in the garden after the last frosts in a light-textured, well-drained soil in full sunlight. Thyme growers usually lime the soil just before the plants are set out. New plants need moisture until they have established a good root system, but second- and subsequent-year plants should only be watered during droughts.

Thyme plants are clipped back during their second year and in later years to force them into a habit of leafy profusion and away from a natural tendency to be woody and sparse of leaf. The more leaves a plant has, the more water it will need.

Every three or four years the plants should be divided and set out anew in the spring, or their fragrance will lessen. In a good site, under thick mulch and good snow cover, thyme will grow as a perennial (except for the fancy variegated types and the creeping thymes) up through zone 4. Gardeners in more frigid or exposed climates should grow their thyme in containers. If you live where the climate is kind (zones 5 to 10), by all means try the creeping thymes, which are beautiful ornamental plants as well as culinary herbs.

CHAPTER 5

CHOICE FRUITS

Banana/Beach Plum

Prickly Pear Cactus/Cranberry

Fig/Gooseberry/Dessert Grape

Medlar/Rose

The fruits that we grow in our gardens are the true measure of excellence. We watch them swell and deepen in color, jealously protect them from the piercing beaks of birds, and urge them toward perfection with daily visits as they mature. We comb garden literature for new recipes for manure teas and aphid-defeating sprays. We try companion planting, hang aluminum pie pans among the peaches, or throw nets over the grapes.

At last the aromatic, deeply-colored fruits are ripe and bursting with honeyed juice. We gather the harvest at the peak of flavor. No market produce can rival the luscious, sweet flavor of fruit from the home garden. Cherry soup, blueberries and cream, black currant pie, pear chutney, peach tart, gooseberry fool and cranberry sauce made from home-grown fruit are indescribably delicious.

The classic end to a dinner made of apples and pears, nuts and cheese is often disappointing when the fruits are immature commercial cultivars. But when we raise fine dessert fruits available in no stores and can serve a nutty, crisp Swaar apple, a Golden Russet or Empire, a Highland pear all juicy melting sweetness with a good local cheddar and a handful of toasted almonds or walnuts, we've arrived at the top. There is simply nothing better.

Banana

(*Musa acuminata*, other species)

Here is one for the heated greenhouse. The most important fruits in the tropics are the bananas and plantains, which are closely related; the latter are usually cooked. Bananas are shipped all over the world, and even the most rural of country stores in cold countries carry bunches of the rich, mellow fruits. It wasn't until the turn of this century that bananas gained their worldwide market, and then only because of the development of the refrigerated banana boat. Modern banana boats are constructed so that gas can be pumped into the holds to kill tropical spiders, snakes, and other creatures that have taken refuge in the clusters.

Bananas have an extraordinary affinity for cream and for other fruit flavors, including the fruit-flavored liqueurs. They are prepared in hundreds of exquisite ways; they can be gently cooked in butter with orange liqueur and brown sugar, then covered with raspberry sauce, or beaten into banana ice cream with pistachio nuts, or made into fritters, added to fruit cups and salads, or just drenched in Jersey cream.

There are about twenty-five species of *Musa*. The leaf sheaths form a trunklike cluster called a pseudostem. The true stem is under the soil. Some of these species are much grown for food in the tropics, and both *acuminata* and *paradisiaca* have many cultivars. Other *Musae* are grown for their spectacular ornmental effect in yard and tropical greenhouse, and one species is grown for its fiber, much used in rope making. *Paradisiaca* is supposedly the real fruit with which the serpent tempted Eve. The edible bananas range in color from yellow to green to red, and most are fragrant and sweet, easily digestible, and rich in potassium, phosphorus, magnesium, the B vitamins, and vitamin C.

Banana cultivation is a horticultural specialty, though many northern gardeners with heated greenhouses are enthusiastic and fascinated with the species. Nothing gives the effect of a tropical climate better than banana trees in the greenhouse. Two cultivars—Cavendish and Cavendish Dwarf—are fairly easy to grow in either zone 10 or the heated greenhouse if a minimum temperature of 70 degrees F and the steamy humidity of about 75 percent can be maintained. Cavendish grows about eight feet tall, and the smaller Dwarf can be grown in a pot. These plants will demand rich soil, good drainage, and weekly application of fertilizer or plant food, as well as twelve to sixteen hours of light a day.

Bananas *must* have warmth and moisture. Fluctuating temperatures and dry air will kill your plant. Bananas are also extremely heavy feeders, and in their native habitat they grow best on rich, alluvial bottomland. If you can supply these essentials that duplicate the moist tropical home of the bananas, you can grow the plants far north in your greenhouse, not only for the decorative tropical effect but for the fresh fruits of cultivars rarely seen in stores.

Propagation of the edible hybrids is by rooted suckers or corms. Gardeners in zone 10 can often grow them outdoors successfully if a suitably rich soil and adequate moisture are available. Some banana cultivars can withstand a touch of frost; the tops of the plant will die back, but new growth will come again if the frost has only been a passing thing. (Curiously enough, bananas are grown on a commercial scale in Iceland in the region of the hot geysers.)

Corms are not shipped to northern addresses by banana stock dealers in cold weather, so plan accordingly. When you get your corms, plant them in ten-inch pots, one to a pot, and water them well, in the moist, warm greenhouse. The sheaths will begin to thrust up out of the soil in three or four weeks. If you can give the plant the heat, food, and moisture that it needs, it will be mature at about fifteen to eighteen months. Some gardeners with limited space allow only one sucker at a time to grow and bear, but this spoils the look of the plant.

Both female and male flowers appear on the same plant, so cross-pollination is not a necessity, and if you have only one banana plant, it will be capable of fruiting successfully. The female flower curves downward from the top of the plant and later develops into clusters of bananas that point upward.

Bananas are cut while they are green and ripened off the tree for the best flavors. The bearing stem will die back after producing fruit. Cut it off to allow a new shoot to grow up.

The Banana Tree, a nursery in Easton, Pennsylvania, specializes in rare tropical plant material for the northern grower. It carries thirty-one banana cultivars, including such delicacies as the Cavendish; Golden Pillow from Southeast Asia; the pink-fleshed Polynesian Haa; the tiny Nino, also called the Honey Banana for its sweetness; and a number of familiar commercial cultivars seen in the markets, as well as half a dozen ornamental types.

Banana Tree also carries the hard-to-find and expensive mercury-vapor growing lights, which are specially designed to duplicate natural daylight for maximum plant growth. These are a must for northern growers.

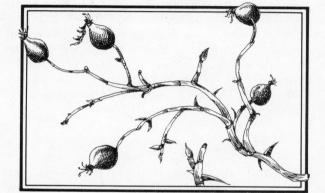

BEACH PLUM

(*Prunus maritima*)

Beach plum jelly has gained an epicurean following so ardent that eating hot popovers with beach plum jelly has become a cult experience. Gardeners need not live on the ocean sand dunes to enjoy the tart treat, for beach plum can be grown inland in many parts of the country.

The sparse fruit grows on straggling little trees along the sandy Atlantic coastline from Maine to Delaware. The trees are bent, both by natural inclination and the beating wind, into interesting shapes. At the shore, the tenacious roots hold the shifting sands in place, and they are often planted for erosion control.

Lately, some nurserymen, sensing vibrations in gardeners that betray a keen desire to eat beach plum jelly, have begun offering *Prunus maritima* stock.

The beach plum is a native American plum. Hybrids have been created by crossing them with stock from three other major plum groups: the European plums, the Middle-East damsons, and the warmth-loving Japanese plums.

Early explorers and settlers in the New World made use of the beach plums and other native plums almost as soon as they landed, but sent home for the more familiar damsons and greengages. One of the earliest comments on beach plums seems to have been a misidentification. Captain John Smith, cruising along the Massachusetts shore, noted on Plum Island "many faire high groves of mulberrie trees," which were probably beach plums.

Beach plums can be propagated by seed, so save the pits from any beach plums you get in autumnal seashore expeditions to Cape Cod. Cuttings are also used and can be either rooted in damp sand or grafted.

Beach plums will tolerate poor soil and locations other than the ocean shore. The little trees have prolific white blossoms in springtime, and if those blossoms are pollinated, they bear small, very tart plums around September after the tree reaches bearing age. Two or more trees are necessary for pollination. Beach plums are hardy to zone 4 in sheltered places and will withstand the ailments that afflict other plums or more pampered stock rather well. However, plum curculio, black knot, brown rot, and nematode infections can damage the trees.

One of the midwestern wild plums—the sand cherry (*P. besseyi*)—is becoming popular in home gardens. It is hardy, and, like the beach plum, makes a superb jelly and can stand wet soils. The sand cherry has its own admirers, perhaps even more fervent than fanciers of beach plums. There is an organization called the Western Sand Cherry Society whose membership is limited to those who have "a deep interest in improving the Western Sandcherry as a rootstock, a hybrid rootstock, a fruit, or as a hybrid fruit."

Plant healthy stock in a good big hole where the roots can stretch out comfortably. Soil should be light, sandy loam. Plant the plum stock at the same depth it grew in the nursery and tamp the soil in among the roots gently as you fill up the hole to avoid air pockets, which harbor harmful bacteria and provide them with good growth conditions. Leave a slight depression in the soil around the tree as a water sink. Water the little tree well after it is planted and water it deeply every week or ten days throughout the season if natural rainfall is insufficient.

Use common sense in pruning the beach plum or any other fruit tree.

Keep the center of the tree somewhat open to let in the sunlight; this both inhibits disease and ripens the fruit. Decrease the bearing wood if necessary to prevent limb breakage from too much fruit and get rid of any diseased or broken or rubbing branches. Do not try to make a beach plum look like an apple tree. The plums have a different shape—bushier, twiggier. Let the tree follow its natural inclination in general shape.

Beach plum stock is available from Southmeadow Fruit Gardens and Miller Nurseries and Kelly Brothers.

PRICKLY PEAR CACTUS

(*Opuntia* subgenus *opuntia*)

In the Southwest the prickly pear cactus, called the nopal, grows wild and free in desert areas. The fruit—large orange-red or purple elongated berries (or "pears") up to three inches long—is enjoyed as both a vegetable and a fruit. The nopals are first boiled, then made into nopalito salad with herb dressing, or sautéed with chile sauce or used in omelets. Some aficionados enjoy them raw, cutting them in half and eating them with a spoon; the raspberry-red interior is sweet and mild and full of small seeds. They are better peeled, livened up with a few drops of lemon juice and served with thick cream. The pulp can be sieved to remove the seeds and made into a delicious and unusual preserve. One occasionally sees prickly pears in specialty markets in the North, and they are common in the Southwest.

Opuntia cacti are native to North and South America, and they grow southward from British Columbia, the Midwest, and Massachusetts to the tip of South America. Some are hardy to minus-45 degrees F, but most prefer warmth and full sunlight.

The subgenus *O. opuntia* is called prickly pear or tuna cactus. These plants have large, showy flowers (beloved of calendar photographers), and, later, the fat fruits in purple, red, or yellow. The nopal is covered with fine, sharp spines that grow in clusters, and these must be removed, obviously, before the things are eaten, unless you are just scooping out the pulp.

The opuntia are hardy, vigorous, and easy to grow in either the rock garden or the pot. They are propagated by cuttings from the joint or stems, or from seed. If you take cuttings from a plant, let them dry in the air until a corky, tough skin forms over the exposed surface, then plant the cuttings shallowly in a sandy bed in the garden, or a sand-filled pot. Opuntia also grows very readily from seed sown in sterilized sandy soil in small pots or flats. The seed germinates in a few days. Seedlings are moved into increasingly larger pots as they grow.

Like other cactus, opuntia needs plenty of water during its growing period from early spring to fall. In their southwestern habitat opuntia enjoy almost daily brief summer rains that sweep down from the mountains in the afternoons. This is the period when the plants blossom and bear fruit. Northern growers can plunge their opuntia, pot and all, into soil with a sandy, loose texture outdoors in summer, bringing them in again as the summer draws to an end. Over the winter, opuntia are more or less dormant and should be kept in a cool place and watered sparingly. Do not let them dry out.

Harvesting prickly pears calls for gloves. The "pears" can be snapped or cut from the main pad.

To prepare prickly pears, impale one of the fruits on a fork and with a sharp knife cut off the clusters of spines just below the skin. The spines can also be singed off over an open gas burner flame. When the fruit is free of spines, scrape away the thin layer of skin from the entire fruit. Slice it into inch-thick pieces, rinse in cold water, and place in a saucepan. Southwestern cooks generally add a pinch of baking soda to the water to reduce the mucilaginous character of the prickly pear, which is not unlike okra. The slices are simmered until tender, about twenty minutes, then they are rinsed in cold water and drained. When they are cool, the nopalitos are used in scores of recipes. Look in cookbooks featuring Mexican and southwestern cooking.

Seed of the prickly pear is available only from J. L. Hudson, which notes that it is very hardy and was collected in Nebraska.

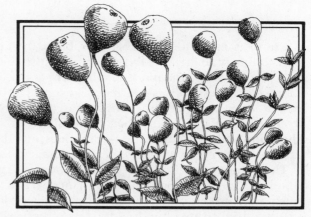

CRANBERRY

(Vaccinium macrocarpon)

He who knows only the supermarket cranberries has never tasted tart cranberry jellies and sauces at their best. Cranberries keep a long time because of their acidity, and the plastic-packaged berries can be months old when you buy them.

The blueberries and cranberries are both among the 150 species of *Vaccinium* shrubs, trees, and vines that are native to North America and northern Europe. The American cranberry is an indigenous plant, a low-growing evergreen shrub with a shallow root system that forms a thick vegetative mat. It is at home in acid bogs and swamps from Newfoundland to North Carolina. Commercial cranberries are nearly all grown in the United States and Canada and shipped abroad, as well as consumed in great quantities here in canned sauces and juice mixtures.

The Indians gathered and used cranberries extensively, often cooking them with maple syrup or honey into a native kind of cranberry sauce. They also pounded them with other berries and nuts and fat into pemmican. The early colonists ate cranberries with enthusiasm, and they were one of the first to be sent back to England as a commercial crop. Waverly Root describes London hawkers crying "Cape Cod bell cranberries" on the Strand in the early eighteenth century.

Cranberries cannot survive outside their extremely acid and boggy environment, where they enjoy a pH of 3.2 to 4.5! They also need substantial amounts of iron as a micronutrient in the soil. It is essential that cranberries grow in water to protect them from winter injury. On drier ground the bushes appear to do well at first, but will suffer winter desiccation, a moisture loss in the leaves that comes when the roots are in frozen earth and unable to draw on a water supply. In the bog, cranberries can take temperatures to minus-50 degrees F, but in drier ground they will be hurt when temperatures are well above zero.

Cranberries are also quite susceptible to frost damage in spring and fall, and commercial growers have elaborate sprinkler systems in their production bogs to spray the plants as the temperature drops. Setting up a commercial cranberry bog is enormously expensive, but once it is established, it can produce heavy crops for more than a century; thirty to fifty years is an average life span. The cranberry's sensitivity to weather and insect pests, the labor-intensive cultivation techniques, and the short harvesting seasons make cranberry growing one of the riskier horticultural enterprises.

The home cook with his or her own bog can establish a small cranberry patch and enjoy the fresh, beautiful, tart berries for generations. Cranberry bushes are prodigiously bountiful, and an acre of commercial bog will give one hundred to two hundred barrels of berries annually. William Rhind puts it all on a smaller scale when he says that in one year, in a space of eighteen square feet, a crop of "three and a half Winchester bushels of berries were produced, which, at five bottles to the gallon, gives 140 bottles, each sufficient for one cranberry pie." (A Winchester bushel is the same as the U.S. standard bushel.)

Cranberry cultivars are strains developed from regional wild plants over the years. Early Black and Howes are much grown in New Jersey and Massachusetts. Searles Jumbo and the new hybrid Stevens are the cranberries of choice with Wisconsin growers, and in the Pacific Northwest and British Columbia they like McFarlin. Many new hybrid cranberries have come into the market in the last few years, most bred for the convenience of commercial growers.

To grow cranberries, first get a bog. Clear the section of bog where you wish them to be, then purchase cuttings. Set the cuttings in rows four feet apart, with six inches between plants. The cranberries will quickly establish their domain by sending out trailing stems. The plants bloom in May, and the fruit is ready in late autumn—October or November.

Mr. Rhind in *The History of the Vegetable Kingdom* gives a slightly different account of growing cranberries at home that may be useful:

> All that is necessary is to drive in a few stakes two or three feet within the margin of the pond, and to place some old boards within these, so as to prevent the soil of the cranberry bed from falling into the water. Then to lay a parcel of small stones or rubbish in the bottom, and over it peat or bog earth, to the depth of about three inches above, and seven inches below the usual surface of the water. In such a situation the plants grow readily; and if a few be put in they entirely cover the bed in the course of a year or two.

The cultivars Stevens, Searles, McFarlin, and Ben Lear are available from Dean Foster Nurseries.

Fig
(*Ficus carica*)

Figs are an easy and deliciously rewarding fruit to grow, so much so that European gardeners who move to harsher climes go to great lengths to have producing fig trees in their yards. The taste of a sun-warmed ripe fig is incomparably better than that of packaged or canned or dried figs.

The colors of figs are variable, from a dark, brown-green to russet yellow to purple, red, and a rich toast-brown. A fig is ripe when its skin seems about to burst and sweet, clear drops form in the cavity at the end of the fruit. Figs are quite perishable. They will not ripen off the tree, and they deteriorate quickly.

In Italy fresh figs are often combined with Pecorino cheese or prosciutto. In Bari, says Waverly Root in his *Best of Italian Cooking*, ripe figs are gently warmed over the fire in a pan with almonds, fennel, and bay leaf. White figs are stuffed with walnuts and almonds, and in Syria a rich fruit salad made of fresh figs and apricots, pine nuts, grapes, and honey is enjoyed as *khoshaf*.

Indeed, figs are one of the great fruits of the world, the major fruit in the ancient Mediterranean countries. They are still important in the cuisine of people living in Greece, Italy, North Africa, and the Middle East. In the ancient world dried figs were an important commodity in trade, and the Romans were decided fig connoisseurs, fancying that the imported figs from Chios and Ibiza were finer than domestic types. That reckless gourmand, Apicius, who squandered his fortune on stunning culinary events, fed pigs with outrageously expensive figs imported from Syria to improve the flavor of the final pork. Later, geese were fed on a rich diet of figs for the sake of their livers, the beginning of *foie gras*.

The fig was one of the earliest domesticated plants, according to horticultural historians, and the reputation of one ancient cultivar, Smyrna fig, has echoed through the ages since they were grown there around 1000 B.C. Smyrna figs are still considered the crème de la crème of the fig world. Fig trees made it to England and France in the sixteenth century, but they were planted in tubs on wheels so that they could be moved inside as winter advanced.

The common fig is a deciduous native of the Mediterranean; it is a handsome plant with glossy leaves, and the succulent, swollen fruits are extremely sweet when ripe. There are many fig cultivars, and a few of them can stand considerable frost, though most are hardy only to zone 8. Warm-region fig cultivars in California, the Mediterranean, South Africa, and Australia are pollinated by the fig wasp, which breeds only in the wild caprifig. Caprifigs are not edible themselves, but are planted among the luscious cultivars for pollination purposes, much as crab apples are planted near certain cultivars of apple. Fortunately, the common fig does not need the attention of this wasp in order to set fruit.

Figs may be grown in a fan shape against a sunny, sheltered wall at the limits of their range, or grown in tubs and shifted inside the cold greenhouse or a cool, dry basement for the winter. Growing figs in tubs restricts root growth and forces the tree to fruit more heavily. Root-pruning is a common procedure with fig trees to urge the plant into better fruit production. A fig tub can be an old whiskey barrel, steam-cleaned and sawed in half, or an expensive redwood plant tub. The tub should be layered at the bottom with rough gravel or stones for good drainage. It is fatal for water to stand around fig roots.

Figs are generally pruned moderately, enough to keep the tree in bounds. Fan-shaped or espaliered figs against a wall need more care, of course, in shaping.

In warm climates figs bear two crops a year, one in summer and a secondary crop in fall, when the fruit is smaller and drier. The second crop is unlikely to ripen in colder climates, and the unripe figs should be removed when they are small and given to the pig or the compost heap rather than letting the tree waste its strength on a crop that will never be eaten.

Dwarf everbearing figs are best suited to tub growing, and they will bear sweet, fat figs nearly as good in quality as the favorite Brown Turkey. The potted dwarf needs full sun, fairly rich soil, mulch, and regular water.

Every gardener has read accounts in the newspapers of skillful Italian gardeners who live in New York City or Boston, yet grow fig trees in their backyards, many hundreds of miles north of their natural range. These trees do not usually give heavy crops, but they do bear fresh figs year after year. The trick is in the old practice of laying the trees down for the winter. Brown Turkey is one of the hardiest figs, and it is often chosen as the subject for this bit of horticultural showmanship.

Fig trees to be laid down in winter are pruned in order to be kept small. In autumn the branches are tied upward into a tidy bundle with horticultural twine that will not cut into the bark. The entire tree is then wrapped in burlap, which is snugly but not tightly tied in place.

A trench about eight inches deep is dug from the base of the tree to a distance that will accommodate its height. Then a circle about two feet out from the trunk is dug around the base of the tree, as though the gardener were root-pruning, which, in fact, he is. The shovel is sharp, and some of the outlying roots are severed. No matter, the fig will profit from this nipping and give more fruit and less foliage. The tree is pried over in the direction of the trench by lifting the root-ball mass on the far side and severing any roots underneath that are holding the ball of earth down. At last the tree will fold over on its remaining roots as though it were hinged and lie in the trench.

Soil is heaped over all parts of the tree, including the root mass, then covered with tar paper and mulch.

In spring the procedure is reversed. After the frosts are past, the soil is carefully removed from the recumbent tree, and it is lifted up, slowly and gently, into its accustomed place. The roots are covered over with good soil and the tree is watered. After the burlap is taken off, the branches are untied and allowed to return to their former position by themselves over the next few weeks. Trying to force the branches into a more horizontal position can break them, so nature is allowed to straighten them out.

Bountiful Ridge carries four fig cultivars, all rated zones 4 to 7. These are the Dwarf everbearing type for pot growing; the widely planted Celeste, which grows fruits with red-violet skins and rose flesh; the well-known Brown Turkey, small in stature, quite hardy, and producing fruit of superior merit; and the Magnolia, a large, golden fig.

GOOSEBERRY

(*Ribes* spp.)

Gooseberry pie, gooseberry fool, gooseberry-elderflower jelly, gooseberry chutney, gooseberry ice cream—all are rare treats in North America, where the gooseberries remain mysterious plants with an evil reputation as hosts of pine blister rust, a disease that attacks and kills white pine. One is warned not to grow gooseberries within nine hundred feet of white pine, and some states forbid the importation of currants and gooseberries, while others insist on signed permits from the county agent. Newer regulations are more relaxed, and interest in the gooseberries is starting to show in the attention breeders and nurseries are giving them.

The finest-flavored gooseberries in the world are grown in Scotland, particularly around Dundee, Aberdeen, and Inverness. The northern counties, cool, moist, and cloudy, suit the gooseberry very well. It is a plant that prefers shade to sun and likes cold, wet weather.

Gooseberries come in a considerable range of sizes and colors. In England more than one thousand cultivars are known, with names like Lancashire, Old Ironmonger, and the like. William Rhind was as staunch a supporter as the gooseberry has ever had, not only because it is a delicious fruit, but also for social and moral reasons. He wrote:

> Any pursuit which makes men acquainted with the peculiarities of vegetable economy, in however small a degree, has a beneficial effect on the heart and understanding; and it is certainly better for weavers and nailers to vie with each other in raising the largest gooseberries, than in those games of chance or cruel sports, to which the few leisure hours of the working classes are too often devoted.

The gooseberries and currants are two distinct groups in the *Ribes* genus, which counts 150 species of low shrubs, mostly native to the Northern Hemisphere. Two among the gooseberries are grown here and in Europe for table use. *R. hirtellum,* the American gooseberry, grows wild from Newfoundland to South Dakota, and has been used to make most of our hybrid crosses. These hybrids are more disease resistant than the European gooseberry, *R. uva-crispa,* but smaller and of less distinguished flavor.

Gooseberry bushes grow to shoulder height but can spread out aggressively. They are not particularly handsome or graceful in form, and their fruit is their main virtue. They are self-fruitful and start bearing at three years. The first few years of production sees the biggest berries, but in later years the smaller berries are more plentiful. An established gooseberry bush can give fine crops of fruit for half a century, though twenty to thirty years is more common. The plants need a rich, heavy, moist soil that is well drained. Mulch and fertilizer high in nitrogen spur gooseberries on tremendously. They are responsive to and grateful for good care.

Gooseberries also have dreadful thorns on their stems, and they are thick and plentiful. One cultivar, the Pixwell (a good pun), has been bred to bear the berries dangling under the branches below the fierce spines. Pixwell is a cultivar from a North Dakota experiment station and has been around since 1932. Most gooseberry pickers wear a glove on the left hand to hold the branch in a good position, and pick gingerly with the right.

Gooseberry culture is not difficult. The plants like a cool environment and will grow on a north wall that gets no sun. They enjoy the same rations of potash and nitrogen as strawberries and their close relatives, the currants. All three of these fruits are often grown together in the same fruit garden. Gooseberries appear on the previous few years' growth, so fall pruning should be careful and slow, not only on account of the thorns, but through deliberation. Weak canes and those more than three years old are cut out.

Cultivars are many in England, but few here. Pink, white, green, yellow, amber, and red are all colors of gooseberries. The big European types are harder to grow than the American hybrids, for they are more susceptible to mildew and other gooseberry ailments. Still, some English cultivars are carried by Southmeadow Fruit Gardens, which lists eleven gooseberries in its pages. The New York State Fruit Testing Cooperative Association carries Fredonia: "probably the best English type as well as being one of the largest," and the American type, Poorman: "the most vigorous, healthiest and most reliably productive of any variety grown at Geneva." Almost every nursery that sends out a catalog with gooseberry listings includes Pixwell. Welcome, Red Jacket and Colossal are hybrids that are listed in several catalogs.

DESSERT GRAPE

(*Vitis* sp.)

Even gardeners who have grown the more difficult vegetables successfully for years sometimes hesitate to try grapes. Millennia of admiration for the vine and the cult of fine wines have enveloped the *Vitis* genus in a mystique that makes it at once alluring and frightening. In the world of flowers the orchid is in a similar position. One opens a book on grape culture to be confronted with pages of diagrams on rival systems of trellises and pruning that look like plans for suspension bridges; there are discussions of flint soils and degrees of vineyard slope, not to mention endless chapters on black rot, powdery and downy mildew, dead-arm, grape-berry moth and red-banded leaf roller. The would-be enthusiast closes the book, takes the order form, and writes "potatoes" on it.

Part of the difficulty is the varied forms of grapes and the vast number of cultivars, which make decisions difficult for the beginner. Picking out the right grape for one's garden, preferred uses, climate, and taste is most of the battle. The best introduction to grapes is to choose a few cultivars that you know you can grow in your region, then add several you want to try. Plant the more tender cultivars against sheltered, sunny walls, or try them in a cold greenhouse.

In North America there are four cultural groups of grapes. American cultivars are hybrids of native species, most involving *Vitis labrusca* in their background; Concord is the best known of these. These cultivars are hardy and quite disease resistant. They are much grown in the Finger Lakes district of New York State. These cultivars include some very fine table grapes and make good wines.

Vitis vinifera grapes are the classic European wine grapes, in this country mostly grown in California, Washington, Oregon, and some of the southwestern states, and in British Columbia. California wines have been of very high quality in the last decades.

French hybrids are crosses between *V. vinifera* and the American cultivars, and these interesting grapes are planted in increasing numbers in
many regions, including the Finger Lakes district. There are some disease
problems with this group, as with the crochety classic wine grapes.

A native southern group, *V. rotundifolia*, is grown in the South for table
and bottle.

Each of these groups, with the exception of *V. vinifera*, includes excellent
eating and wine grapes. A few extraordinary cultivars make both good desserts and good wine.

There are a number of serious virus diseases that afflict grapes, and the
home gardener is wise to seek out healthy, clean rootstock free from viruses.
Look for virus-indexed grape stock, which is propagated from rootstock
that is certified free of viruses such as fan leaf virus, tobacco and tomato
ring spot, fleck, leaf roll, corky bark, and others. The New York State Fruit
Testing Cooperative Association has been involved for decades in one of the
largest and most extensive programs in grape breeding and testing in the
country. They offer virus-indexed grape stock to their members at reason-
able prices, sometimes lower than inferior stock from other sources. They
list thirty cultivars of dessert grapes, both American and French hybrids,
grouped by ripening dates from very early to late. These include such wonderful grapes as Buffalo, a black, spicy slipskin with a rich, fruity aroma and
flavor; Seneca, a very sweet, winey white table grape with European ancestors; Alwood, a blue-black sweet Concord type that ripens several weeks
before Concord; and the fine white Ontario, firm, sweet, and fine-grained in
texture. Buffalo is a multi-purpose grape that is delicious out of hand and
makes an excellent wine.

Among a dozen seedless grapes—crosses between *V. vinifera* and hardy
American types—are some of the most delicious of all table grapes. Himrod
is the finest of these, in my opinion—loose clusters of sweet yellow grapes
with a rich, fruity fragrance and savor and crisp, juicy flesh. Canadice, an
offspring of Himrod × Bath, is the easiest of the seedless grapes to grow.

The Association also sells French hybrids that are both fine dessert grapes
and a source of superior wines, often blended. Aurore, Seibel 13047, Verde-
let, and Villard Blanc are all excellent for table or wine. The Association also
carries six of the classic *V. vinifera* wine grapes.

It is the gardener's great good luck that grapevines can be grown on many
soils as long as the drainage of both water and air is good. Deep, sandy
loams are the best soils, for grapevines will put down tremendous roots (as
anyone who has tried to pull one up knows). A frost-free period of *at least* 150
days is necessary for the American cultivars, and a longer period of 180 days

is far better. Do not go entirely by zone maps. Consult your experience and knowledge of your best possible sites, check your garden records for temperature averages, and select the best microclimate on your property for the grapevines. Full sun, shelter, well-drained soil, and a position upslope from frost pockets are necessary for good grape culture.

The rootstock should be planted in spring in a good-size hole with sifted soil worked carefully into the roots to prevent air pockets. In the Northeast, grape plants are set about eight feet apart in the row. After American vines are planted, they are cut back to two or three plump buds on the main stem. Coarse mulching material is spread over the soil to keep erosion and weed growth in check, and the plants are watered. When the buds begin to grow, only the two strongest are kept. Nip the others off.

The first season the young grapes spend in your vineyard they may be staked for support. Any flower clusters should be cut off. Do not be tempted to "just see what they're like"—you'll do years of damage to the struggling young vines. The strength of the plant must go into a good root system. Otherwise, the plants are kept weeded and given water once a week or so, but allowed to grow freely. You can set the eight-foot posts you will need next year to support the vines. Set them thirty inches deep, midway between the plants and one at each end. Two lengths of number-10 wire are strung along the posts, the bottom wire two feet above the ground, the top wire five feet above the ground.

If you live in a northern climate, arbors probably sound attractive to you, but they are not a good idea, no matter how enticing the prospect of plucking ripe clusters from a shaded seat beneath the arching vines. It is better to grow the vines on a simple two-wire fence (the Four-Arm Kniffen system), for this allows you to recline tender vines gently on the ground in autumn and heap earth over them. Tedious as this chore may sound, it is the only way gardeners in the North can keep the more delicate grapes going.

In the second spring, before the buds break, visit your grape vines with scissors in hand and cut the plants back to a single stem without any branches. Do this before the sap rises in the vine and before the buds swell. Then, during the summer as the buds on the stem grow into canes, allow two on each side of the main stem to grow; two for the lower wire, two for the upper wire. The vine will look as though it is stretching out two sets of arms to the right and to the left. These arms will be next year's fruit-bearing canes. In the autumn, in cold northern climates, untie and gently bring the vine down to earth level and cover it over again with soil.

In the third spring, you can look forward to the first fruits of your labor. Be sure to resurrect your vines if you have buried them. Last year's canes are this year's bearing wood, but once the grapes have been picked, the canes are no longer good. Four more arms must be grown to replace them, and they are coached along early in the season before the main arms have borne their fruit. The main stem obligingly supplies more buds. Choose the new four that will be next year's bearing wood, and allow them to grow parallel to the fruiting canes. In the autumn, after the plant is dormant, cut off the old bearing canes. The next spring you will tie up the new canes you allowed to grow and start four new ones to replace them.

Basically that is it for the next fifty years. Keep growing and working in new canes, and cutting out the ones that bore in the season just past.*

Tender grapes can also be grown in a cold greenhouse if you have such a luxury. There is no heat in such a greenhouse. This was a favorite horticultural feat of the Victorians. Often the roots were outdoors in the earth, and the stem and arms inside, protected from frost and wind. Inside support for the vines is provided by number-10 wire running the length of the greenhouse and strung through eyebolts every six feet or so. The arms of the vines can be trained on the wires by any system you like to use. Good ventilation is crucial, especially in summer when the greenhouse heats up, for mildew is a serious disease of grapes and the risk is much greater when the vines are enclosed. In their natural habitat (or if left to their own devices) grapes will climb high into the tops of trees where the wind sweeps them clean.

Table grapes should be picked on a dry day when the fruit is thoroughly ripe. If they are intended for a simple dessert, a handsome way to present them is to rinse them in cold water, then chill them in the refrigerator for an hour or so and serve them as separate bunches on fine plates whose color will set off the grapes. A few grape leaves can be included for garnish.

The New York State Fruit Testing Cooperative Association offers virus-indexed grape stock of fifty-six cultivars, some of them promising experimental cultivars that have not yet been named or released. Members report back to the Association on problems or successes with their experimental stock and comment on flavor and ripening dates in their area. This is one of the few ways private gardeners and growers can have a say about the fruits later released to the public and commercial growers. Southmeadow carries fifty-five grape cultivars, most of them the American type. Some are rare cultivars impossible to find elsewhere.

Grape Leaves

The young (but full-grown) and relatively tender leaves of species other than *V. vinifera* can be used for dolmas and other grape-leaf-wrapped foods.

---

*French hybrids are pruned differently, as are muscadines. All the side branches are cut back each autumn to two buds. Each bud will grow in the next season to produce fruit. This procedure is called spur pruning.

In Europe the leaves of wine grapes are brined and used as the outer wrapper for pungent and spicy mixtures of meat, vegetables, and rice in Greek, Balkan, North African, and Middle Eastern cooking. Brined leaves can be bought here in specialty stores. But here some gardeners with a grapevine or two cut a number of the largest leaves in early summer or late spring, blanch them, and freeze them in packets of a dozen for stuffing later. The color and flavor of these frozen leaves are superior to the brined ones.

Fresh vine leaves are easy to prepare for stuffing. Pick them large but young, rinse well, and drop them into a few inches of boiling water to which the juice of half a lemon has been added. After a minute take them out. Stuff and roll them according to your recipe. In New Mexico and Arizona, cooks make a very fine dish of quail wrapped in fresh vine leaves and broiled al fresco over mesquite or juniper coals.

Southerners suffer as much anxiety growing grapes as do northerners, but for different reasons. Humidity and mildew, Pierce's disease, and pests kill or cripple most American, French hybrid, or *V. vinifera* grapes attempted in the South. The solution is to grow the native grape, the excellent muscadines, chiefest of which is the scuppernong. *Vitis rotundifolia* is a vigorous climbing grapevine native to the South that has many regional cultivars. The exuberantly growing vines are of the spur type, rather than canes. The clusters are small, but the grapes themselves are large, dull, purple berries. The flavor is unique—sweet, musky, and rich. The first ripe scuppernongs I ever tasted were from William Park's vines in Greenwood, South Carolina, and they were delicious. A single vine can produce about two bushels of grapes each year for up to a century. The fruit makes an excellent jelly, a distinctive juice, and the famous scuppernong wine, a regional delicacy of considerable reputation.

The muscadine cultivars are generally divided into two groups—those that will do best in the Deep South: Magnolia, Magoon, and Welder; and those that flourish in the northern limits of the region up to Tennessee and Virginia: Sterling, Noble, Scuppernong, and Carlos.

The vines are planted fifteen to twenty feet apart and can be trained in any system the gardener prefers or made into an arbor. It is probably not a bad idea to let a vine or two climb into a low tree. (This was the ancient Italian way of growing grapes.) Tree-climbing vines are not so convenient, but look grand and attract birds.

If you decide to make a muscadine arbor, use sturdy, unpainted timbers that have been treated with a preservative, or galvanized pipes set in concrete, for the supports. Timbers treated with creosote or pentachlorophenol are toxic to plants, so try to get salts-treated timbers preserved with chromated copper arsenate or ammoniacal copper arsenate and be quite careful that the roots of the vines do not enter the ground near these posts, for some gardeners report that their plants are less vigorous when the root systems are in contact with salts-treated posts. A muscadine vine lasts for a long time, and each weighs hundreds of pounds when loaded with foliage and fruit. Many an arbor has crumbled and rotted away beneath its vine.

Suppliers of muscadine stock are:

Hastings
Box 4274
Atlanta, Georgia 30302

Isons Nursery and Vineyard
Brooks, Georgia 30205

Bountiful Ridge Nurseries, Inc.
Princess Anne, Maryland 21853

MEDLAR

(*Mespilus germanica*)

The medlar is the only species in the genus *Mespilus*, a rather lonely classification for this unusual fruit. Medlars were once considered very choice, but that was long ago when tastes were different. Yet their reputation as a special delight still persists, and less than two decades ago Angelo Pellegrini wrote in his *Food-Lover's Garden*, as he inventoried the unusual fruit trees and perennial vegetables and fruits, "I now hope to add a medlar tree, *Mespilus germanica*, to my group of exotics. It is a small, malaceous tree, related to the loquat. Its fruit resembles the crab apple and is edible only in the early stages of decay. I shall have one quite soon—and it will grow for my sake."

The medlar tree is small, and some cultivars take an interesting, torment-
ed shape with branches that seem to writhe and twist; this habit makes it a
desirable ornamental in the garden, particularly in winter against the
snow. The medlar is at home all across southeastern Europe and into Asia
Minor. But it will survive and bear fruit in damp, poor soil in harsher climates as well. Though the small brown fruits will ripen on the tree in Italy,
in England and colder environments in North America they do not. Medlars
in England were customarily picked on a dry day in October after the first
frost and laid on clean straw to "blett," or rot. When at last the fruits were
dark and soft, they were eaten; the flavor has been described as vinous and
sweet and as possessing "an agreeable acidity." Traditionally these soft
fruits accompanied a glass of port wine. Modern medlar eaters prefer to
blend the pulp with cream and custard for medlar mousse. A very nice jelly
of transparent amber-orange color is made from medlars that are not entirely ripe.

In the nineteenth century, one of the most esteemed medlar cultivars was
Nottingham, which made a small tree that bore small fruits of very good
flavor. The common Dutch medlars, says William Rhind, were inferior in
flavor. Nottingham is still available from the only medlar source in North
America, Southmeadow Fruit Gardens.

Plant Nottingham with the graft union below the soil for sturdier root
support. The trees are fairly trouble-free and slow-growing; they make a
hard, dense wood. Medlars are hardy in the North if they are grown in a
sheltered, sunny place with good drainage. They will survive in damp, mis-
erable locations, but fruit quality will be poorer and the quantity less than if
they were given every advantage.

Medlar stock is generally grafted onto quince, hawthorne, or pear rootstock, and you may wish to propagate your medlars thus for neighbors and
gardening friends who might appreciate such a curiosity. Dwarf medlars
are almost always grafted onto quince, and they make a small tree scarcely
larger than a bush.

Prune medlars to an open center that lets sunlight in to the fruit for the
first three or four years. Subsequent pruning, once the basic form is established, simply checks out-of-bounds growth.

After the first frost, gather the medlars and store them in a cool, clean area
with their stems upright. The fruits should not touch each other. In three
weeks they will be soft and brown and look quite far gone to lovers of fresh
fruit, but they are now sweet and soft and ready to eat.

ROSE

(*Rosa spp.*)

Nearly two decades ago rosarian Jean Gordon wrote a fine little book called *The Art of Cooking with Roses* (New York; Noonday Press, 1968). This work contained scores of rose recipes used in Europe and the Orient and by our ancestors throughout the nineteenth century, including subtle and delicious rose flavorings in honey, creams, sauces, pastries, and unusual delicacies.

Rose syrup is a necessary ingredient in baklava, that melting, rich, Eastern pastry composed of tissue-thin layers of phyllo dough. When the baklava has baked to a light gold and the chopped pistachio nuts and almonds on the top a darker, nutty brown, it is removed tenderly from the oven and sprinkled with rose syrup or the lighter rose water. Fruit dumplings and steamed puddings are ennobled with honey rose sauce, that melting mixture of cream, honey, butter, and rose water. Rose-flavored Bavarian Cream with crushed raspberries is a poem. Rose flavoring is used for entrées also, with pork chops and pineapple, in fruit pancakes. Rose ice cream is a unique and exquisitely delicious dessert, especially when garnished with *Rosa rugosa* blooms. Rose-flavored butter for popovers, hot biscuits, and muffins and rose-scented honey are rarities for the Sunday brunch tray. Pickled rosebuds go into salads. White wine vinegar or cider vinegar can be flavored with rose petals. Fragrant rose blossom tea, used in the Far East to honor special guests, is made by steeping the dried petals. Honey-glazed chicken entrées in the style of the Middle East are made fragrant with rose water in the glaze. A Greek dish of stewed lamb on a bed of rice is seasoned with the subtle fragrance of rose water. Squash, fish, carrots, beets, pies and cakes, puddings, all can be touched lightly with the perfume of the rose.

Rose water and rose syrups are sold in some specialty food stores, but they can be made at home in a few hours. Not so simple to make is rose extract, a fabulously expensive distillate of rose oils usually imported from Bulgaria where fragrant roses are a major crop. In India, Turkey, and Egypt a bottle of rose water stands on the table as do ketchup bottles in American diners.

Rose cultivars vary in flavors and perfumes as much as apples do. The Cinnamon Rose, the Damask Rose, the Hundred Leaf Rose—all have their distinctive fragrances. As a rule of thumb, the dark-red roses are more strongly flavored than the pale tints. Many modern roses are not fragrant, but a new interest in fine-scented flowers has brought our attention back to the many exquisitely perfumed roses of culinary quality. Rose dealers offer many fragrant roses today. Information on rose culture and a handbook to guide the rosarian in selecting the roses suited to a certain climate and interest can be had from the American Rose Society, P.O. Box 30,000, Shreveport, Louisiana 71130. This is one of the most active plant societies in North America, with hundreds of local groups of rose fanciers.

The roses of greatest interest to the kitchen gardener are the *rugosas*, the *gallicas*, and the *albas*.

The *Rugosa* came originally from China and Japan, but it now grows all over the world, very often along the seacoast, where the hardy plant will stand the wind and weather. These strong plants can be grown as thick hedges. These are the roses often seen growing against the faded cedar shingles of cottages on the Maine coast. The single roses are large and extremely fragrant, with big orange hips to be gathered for teas and infusions. The colors range from white to shell pink to blushing mauve to a splendid red.

Rosa gallica was the common ancestor of all the roses known in Europe until *rugosa* was introduced in the eighteenth century. These beautiful things included damask roses, and all the *gallicas* seem drenched in a heavy, rich perfume that makes the head swim. Their extraordinary colors caused them to be known as "the mad *gallicas*"; they range from a melting violet pink through purple mauves into dark wine. Some cultivars show a pearly-pale-gray color on the backs of the petals.

Alba blooms once a year, in late spring. The flowers are pale pink to white, with a distinctive, very rich fragrance that seems to lie palpably on the air. The large plants are known for their gray-green foliage.

There are other varieties also worthy of your attention. *Portland* roses are very hard to find these days, but they are worth the search, for they are the offspring of the autumn damask roses, with a deep, sweet scent. The *Bourbon* roses are a dark pink, and never fully open, but keep a cupped petal shape. They were favorite subjects when ladies painted flowers on china plates. Forced hothouse roses have no culinary use.

A scarce book that is a real find for the rose fancier is Alice Morse Earle's *Sun-Dials and Roses of Yesterday*, published in 1902 and full of lore about the old fragrant roses.

One way to make *rose water* is with a very simple kitchen still. Don't use a pressure cooker—it's too dangerous. Instead, use a large teakettle, three or four feet of 1/4-inch copper tubing, a rubber baby's bottle nipple small enough at the base to fit snugly over the teakettle spout, a big kettle of cold water, and a clean pint jar.

Fill the teakettle half full of water. Strew handfuls of fragrant fresh rose petals thickly over the water. Put on the lid.

Cut a small slit in the tip of the nipple and work in one end of the copper tubing. The rubber should be snug around the tubing. Draw the nipple over the teakettle spout.

Bend the copper tubing so that it descends to the floor where you have set the kettle of cold water and, beside it, the clean pint jar. Bend the tubing so that it dips into the cold-water bath and out again, over the lip of the kettle and into the clean pint jar.

Turn the heat on low under the rose-petal kettle. The steam that rises from the kettle will pass into the copper tube, redolent with rose-oil fragrance. When this steam passes through the section of copper tubing that is in the cold-water kettle, it condenses and trickles into the pint jar as rose water.

Keep the finished rose water tightly capped in a cool, dark place. Use it in cooking just before serving to prevent the elusive fragrance from dissipating. The greatest number of recipes calling for rose water are in cookbooks specializing in cuisine of the Near and Middle East. Gordon's *The Art of Cooking with Roses* is out of print and may be found through rare-book dealers specializing in cookery books.

ROSE MEASUREMENTS

1 pound of rose petals equals 11 cups

1 pound of rose hips equals 4 cups

Rose honey is made easily by pounding a cup of fragrant rose petals in a mortar, then scraping the pulp into a small stainless-steel saucepan. Pour one cup of mild honey, such as orange blossom, over the crushed petals and warm over low heat for two or three minutes, or until the honey runs thinly. Strain the honey back into its jar and let it stand a week or so before using.

To make *rose jelly*, add fragrant whole rose petals during the last stages of making apple jelly, before the jelly begins to sheet. Strain the hot jelly through a stainless-steel strainer into sterilized jars and seal.

Swiss rose-hip jams and *Swedish rose-hip soup* with Madeira and whipped cream garnished with shredded almonds are a natural part of the cuisine when there is a rose garden outside the kitchen door. The hips of *rugosa* are particularly large and good.

There are few pleasures as keen as dining on the fruits of your own garden, and that pleasure is intensified when the cultivars are choice, unusually delicious, or demanding to grow. The harvested fruits are then an achievement, and the meal a gustatory experience that will be remembered for a long time. Your table and your dinner guests are honored by such rare fare, and you, the gardener-cook, can be well satisfied that it is the best that there is.

SOURCES

SOURCES OF SEEDS

Bountiful Gardens
5798 Ridgewood Road
Willits, California 95490

The Cook's Garden
Box 65053
Londonderry, Vermont 05148

Country Herbs
Stockbridge, Massachusetts 01262

William Dam Seeds Ltd.
P.O. Box 8400
Dundas, Ontario, Canada L9H 6M1

J.A. Demonchaux Co., Inc.
827 North Kansas St.
Topeka, Kansas 66608

Elysian Hills
RFD #1
Dummerston, Brattleboro,
Vermont 05301

Greenleaf Seeds
P.O. Box 89
Conway, Massachusetts 01341

Greenwood Nursery
2 El Camino Real
Goleta, California 93117

Harris Seeds
Moreton Farm
3670 Buffalo Rd.
Rochester, New York 14624

Horticultural Enterprises
P.O. Box 340082
Dallas, Texas 75234-0082

J. L. Hudson, Seedsman
P.O. Box 1058
Redwood City, California 94064

Le Jardin du Gourmet
West Danville, Vermont 05873

Johnny's Selected Seeds
Albion, Maine 04901

K & L Cactus Company
12712 Stockton Blvd.
Galt, California 95632
($2 catalog)

Kerncraft
434 West Main St.
Kutztown, Pennsylvania 19530

Kitazawa Seed Co.
356 West Taylor St.
San Jose, California 95110

Le Marché
P.O. Box 566
Dixon, California 95620

Liberty Seed Co.
Box 806
New Philadelphia, Ohio 44663

Mellinger's
2310 W. South Range Rd.
North Lima, Ohio 44452-9731

Nichols Garden Nursery
1109 North Pacific Highway
Albany, Oregon 97321

Park Seed Co.
Highway 254 North
Greenwood, South Carolina 29647

Seed Savers Exchange
203 Rural Avenue
Decorah, Iowa 52101
(members only; $10 annually)

Seeds Blum
Idaho City Stage
Boise, Idaho 83706

Shady Hill Gardens
753 Walnut St.
Batavia, Illinois 60510
(scented geraniums)

Shepherd's Garden Seeds
7389 West Zayante Rd.
Felton, California 95018

Stokes Seeds
Box 548
Buffalo, New York 14624

Suffolk Herbs
Sawyers Farm, Little Cornard
Sudbury, Suffolk, England

Thompson and Morgan
P.O. Box 100
Farmingdale, New Jersey 07727

William Tricker
7125 Tanglewood Avenue
Independence, Ohio 44131

or

74 Allendale Avenue
Saddle River, New Jersey 07458

Tsang & Ma
P.O. Box 294
Belmont, California 94002

Three Springs Fisheries
Lilypons, Maryland 21717

The Urban Farmer, Inc.
P.O. Box 22198
Beachwood, Ohio 44122

Van Ness Water Gardens
2460 North Euclid Avenue
Upland, California 91786

Vermont Bean Seed Co.
Garden Lane
Bomoseen, Vermont 05732

SOURCES OF PLANTS

The Banana Tree
715 Northampton St.
Easton, Pennsylvania 18042

Bountiful Ridge Nurseries, Inc.
Princess Anne, Maryland 21853

Dean Foster Nurseries
Hartford, Michigan 49057

Fedco Trees
Box 340
Palermo, Maine 04354

Kelly Brothers
Dansville, New York 14437

Miller Nurseries
Canandaigua, New York 14424

New York State Fruit Testing
Cooperative Association, Inc.
Geneva, New York 14456

Southmeadow Fruit Gardens
2363 Tilbury Place
Birmingham, Michigan 48009

Square Root Nursery,
The Grape People
4764 Deuel Rd.
Canandaigua, New York 14424

Stark Brothers Nurseries
Louisiana, Missouri 63353

SOURCES OF EQUIPMENT, TOOLS, AND GADGETS

Green River Tools
5 Cotton Mill Hill
P.O. Box 1919
Brattleboro, Vermont 05301
(Soil block implements, etc.)

Mellinger's
2310 West South Range Street
North Lima, Ohio 44452
(Shade cloths, etc.)

Smith and Hawken
25 Corte Madera
Mill Valley, California 94941
(All kinds of tools, including
 scaled-down versions)

Walt Nicke
Box 667
Hudson, New York 12534
(Cloches, etc.)

BIBLIOGRAPHY

All About Growing Fruits and Berries. San Francisco: Ortho Books, 1976.

Baker, Margaret. *Discovering the Folklore of Plants*. Aylesbury, Bucks.: Shire Publications Ltd., 1969, 1980.

Beckett, Kenneth. *The Gardener's Bedside Book*. London: B.T. Batsford Ltd., 1973

Calvin, Clyde L., and Knutson, Donald. *Modern Home Gardening*. New York: John Wiley and Sons, 1983.

Chan, Peter, and Gill, Spencer. *Better Vegetable Gardens the Chinese Way: Peter Chan's Raised-Bed System*. Portland, Oregon: Graphic Arts Center, 1977.

Creasy, Rosalind. *The Complete Book of Edible Landscaping*. San Francisco: Sierra Club Books, 1982.

Dahlen, Martha, and Phillipps, Karen. *A Popular Guide to Chinese Vegetables*. New York: Crown Publishers, Inc., 1983.

Earle, Alice Morse. *Sun Dials and Roses of Yesterday*. New York: Macmillan, 1902.

The Encyclopedia of Organic Gardening. Emmaus, Pennsylvania: Rodale Press, 1978.

Flawn, Louis N. *Gardening With Cloches*. London: John Gifford Ltd., 1957, 1967.

Foster, Gertrude B., and Louden, Rosemary F. *Park's Success with Herbs*. Greenwood, South Carolina: Geo. W. Park Seed Co., Inc., 1980.

Gessert, Kate Rogers. *The Beautiful Food Garden*. New York: Van Nostrand Reinhold, 1983.

Gordon, Jean. *The Art of Cooking with Roses*. New York: Noonday Press, 1968.

Halpin, Anne Moyer, ed. *Gourmet Gardening*. Emmaus, Pennsylvania: Rodale Press, 1978, 1981.

Haydock, Yukio, and Haydock, Bob. *Japanese Garnishes: The Ancient Art of Mukimono*. New York: Holt, Rinehart, Winston 1980.

Hill, Lewis. *Fruits and Berries for the Home Garden*. New York: Alfred A. Knopf, 1977.

Hortus Third. New York: Macmillan Publishing Company, 1976.

Jabs, Carolyn. *The Heirloom Gardener*. San Francisco: Sierra Club Books, 1984.

Jeavons, John. *How to Grow More Vegetables*. Berkeley: Ten Speed Press, 1979.

Larkcom, Joy. *The Salad Garden*. New York: Viking Press, 1984.

Leighton, Anne. *Early American Gardens*. Boston: Houghton Miffin Company, 1970.

Norman, Barbara. *Tales of the Table*. Englewood, New Jersey: Prentice-Hall, 1972.

Parkinson, John. *Paradisi in Sole, Paradisus Terrestris*. 1629. Reprint Edition. Walter J. Johnson, 1975.

Pellegrini, Angelo M. *The Food-Lover's Garden*. New York: Alfred A. Knopf, 1970.

Pépin, Jacques. *La Technique*. New York: Times Books, 1976.

Pomona. Quarterly of the North American Fruit Explorers. 1982–1984.

Powell, Thomas, and Powell, Betty. *The Avant Gardener*. Boston: Houghton Mifflin Company, 1975.

Radecka, Helen. *The Fruit and Nut Book*. New York: McGraw-Hill, 1984.

Reilly, Ann. *Park's Success with Seeds*. Greenwood, South Carolina: Geo. W. Park Seed Co., Inc., 1978.

Rhind, William H. *A History of the Vegetable Kingdom*. Glasgow: Blackie and Sons, 1855.

Root, Waverly. *Food*. New York: Simon and Schuster, 1980.

Shewell-Cooper, W.E. *Herbs, Salads and Tomatoes*. London: John Gifford Ltd., 1961.

Simon, André L. *A Concise Encyclopedia of Gastronomy: Vegetables*. London: Wine and Food Society, 1941, 1948.

Sturtevant, E. Lewis. *Sturtevant's Edible Plants of the World*. Edited by U.P. Hedrick. Reprint edition. New York: Dover Publications, 1972.

Sunset New Western Garden Book. Menlo Park, California: Lane Publishing Company, 1981.

Thrower, Percy. *Fresh Vegetables and Herbs from Your Garden*. New York: Crescent Books, 1974.

Truax, Carol. *The Art of Salad Making*. Garden City, New York: Doubleday & Company, 1968.

Vilmorin-Andrieux. *The Vegetable Garden*. Berkeley: Ten Speed Press, 1981.

Wason, Betty. *The Art of Vegetable Cooking*. New York: Ace Publishing, 1965.

INDEX

C

E

Earle, Alice Morse, 177
English thyme, 151
Evelyn, John, 72, 74
Exotic vegetables
  asparagus, 90–96
  cardoon, 97–99
  celtuce, 100–101
  chiles, 101–3
  globe artichoke, 86–90
  jicama, 103–4
  kudzu, 105
  lotus root, 106–7
  pumpkin, 110–12
  rampion, 113–14
  scorzonera, 118–20
  sea kale, 120–24
  shiitake mushroom, 108–10
  sorrel, 124–26
  tomatillo, 114–16
  tronchuda cabbage, 96–97
  wild rice, 116–17

F

Figs, 163–65
  fig tub, 164
  growing guidelines, 164–65
  historical view, 163–64
  ripeness factor, 163
  seed houses for ordering, 165
Flawn, Louis N., 26
Flowering kales, 54
  growing guidelines, 54
  seed houses for ordering, 54
  varieties of, 54
Fluid sowing, 34–35
  fluid-gel system, 35
  Legume-Aid, 35
Forcing/spring radishes, 74–75
Foster, Gertrude, 130, 132, 142
French intensive gardening, 21–23

French tarragon, 150
French thyme, 151
Fruits
  bananas, 155–57
  beach plums, 157–59
  cranberries, 161–63
  dessert grape, 168–73
  figs, 163–65
  gooseberry, 166–68
  medlar, 173–74
  prickly pear cactus, 159–60
  rose, 175–78

G

Gallicas, rose, 176
Gardena sprinklers, 42
Garden bench, 46
Gardening styles, 20–27
  biodynamic/French intensive
    gardening, 21–23
  Chinese intensive gardening, 23
  cloche gardening, 25–27
  container gardening, 24
  high-density gardening, 21
  organic gardening, 21
  raised beds, 23
  sheet-plastic gardening, 24–25
  vertical gardening, 24
  wide rows, 24
Gardening techniques
  companion planting, 19, 22
  composing, 15–16
  crop rotation, 17–19
  cultivars, choosing, 27–30
  gardening styles, 20–27
  garden plans, 16–17
  garden site, choosing, 4–6
  germination, 33
  mulching, 40–41
  organic material, adding, 9–10
  seed starting, 30–35
  tools/gadgets, 41–46

ABOUT THE AUTHOR

E. Annie Proulx is an experienced gardener and
a lifelong student of garden arts and design. Her highly
varied interests also include cooking, at which she
is expert, and travel. She is an award-winning
writer of both fiction and nonfiction. Her work on
the subject of gardening frequently appears in the
pages of *Horticulture* magazine. She lives
and writes in Vershire, Vermont.